Hobomok

Lydia Child

Table of Contents

Hobomok..1

    Lydia Child..1

    PREFACE...2

    CHAP. I...3

    CHAP. II..12

    CHAP. III...19

    CHAP. IV...26

    CHAP. V..31

    CHAP. VI...37

    CHAP. VII..45

    CHAP. VIII...51

    CHAP. IX...55

    CHAP. X..60

    (*)CHAP. XI...69

    CHAP. XII..73

    CHAP. XIII...79

    CHAP. XIV...88

    CHAP. XV..93

    CHAP. XVI...99

    CHAP. XVII..105

    CHAP. XVIII...111

    CHAP. XIX...119

    CHAP. XX..125

Hobomok

Lydia Child

Kessinger Publishing reprints thousands of hard–to–find books!

Visit us at http://www.kessinger.net

- PREFACE.
- CHAP. I.
- CHAP. II.
- CHAP. III.
- CHAP. IV.
- CHAP. V.
- CHAP. VI.
- CHAP. VII.
- CHAP. VIII.
- CHAP. IX.
- CHAP. X.
- (*)CHAP. XI.
- CHAP. XII.
- CHAP. XIII.
- CHAP. XIV.
- CHAP. XV.
- CHAP. XVI.
- CHAP. XVII.
- CHAP. XVIII.
- CHAP. XIX.
- CHAP. XX.

```
HOBOMOK, A TALE OF EARLY TIMES. BY AN AMERICAN.
Then all this youthful paradise around,
And all the broad and boundless mainland, lay
Cooled by the interminable wood, that frowned
O'er mount and vale.
    — Bryant
```

PREFACE.

IN the summer of 1823, my friend ******* entered my study with an air which indicated he had something to communicate.

"Frederic," says he, "do you know I have been thinking of a new plan lately?"

"A wise one, no doubt," replied I; "but, prithee, what is it?"

"Why, to confess the truth, your friend P*******'s remarks concerning our early history, have half tempted me to write a New England novel."

"A novel!" quoth I—"when Waverly is galloping over hill and dale, faster and more successful than Alexander's conquering sword? Even American ground is occupied. 'The Spy' is lurking in every closet,—the mind is every where supplied with 'Pioneers' on the land, and is soon likely to be with 'Pilots' on the deep."

"I know that," replied he; "Scott wanders over every land with the same proud, elastic tread—free as the mountain breeze, and majestic as the bird that bathes in the sunbeams. He must always stand alone—a high and solitary shrine, before which minds of humbler mould are compelled to bow down and worship. I did not mean," added he, smiling, "that my wildest hopes, hardly my wildest wishes, had placed me even within sight of the proud summit which has been gained either by Sir Walter Scott, or Mr. Cooper. I am aware that the subject which called forth your friend's animated observations, owed its romantic coloring almost wholly to his own rich imagination. Still, barren and uninteresting as New England history is, I feel there is enough connected with it, to rouse the dormant energies of my soul; and I would fain deserve some other epitaph than that 'he lived and died.' "

I knew that my friend, under an awkward and unprepossessing appearance, concealed more talents than the world was aware of. I likewise knew that when he once started in the race, "the de'il take the hindmost" was his favorite motto. So I e'en resolved to favor the project, and to procure for him as many old, historical pamphlets as possible.

A few weeks after, my friend again entered my apartment, and gave me a package, as he said, "Here are my MSS., and it rests entirely with you, whether or not to give them to the public. You, and every one acquainted with our earliest history, will perceive that I owe many a quaint expression, and pithy sentence, to the old and forgotten manuscripts of those times.

"The ardour with which I commenced this task, has almost wholly abated.

"Seriously, Frederic, what chance is there that I, who so seldom peep out from 'the loop–holes of retreat,' upon a gay and busy world, can have written any thing which will meet their approbation? Besides, the work is full of faults, which I have talents enough to see, but not to correct. It has indeed fallen far short of the standard which I had raised in my own mind. You well know that state of feeling, when the soul fixes her keen vision on distant brightness, but in vain stretches her feeble and spell–bound wing, for a flight so lofty. The world would smile," continued he, "to hear me talk thus, concerning a production, which will probably never rise to the surface with other ephemeral trifles of the day;—but painful, anxious timidity must unavoidably be felt by a young author in his first attempt. However, I will talk no more about it. 'What is writ, is writ—would it were worthier.'

"If I succeed, the voice of praise will cheer me in my solitude. If I fail, thank Heaven, there is no one, but yourself, can insult me with their pity."

Perhaps the public may think me swayed by undue partiality,—but after I had read my friend's MS. I wrote upon the outside, "Send it to the Printer."

CHAP. I.

```
How daur ye try sic sportin,
As seek the foul thief ony place,
For him to spae your fortune?
Nae doubt but ye may get a sight!
Great cause ye hae to fear it;
For mony a ane has gotten a fright,
An' liv'd and died deleeret.

     — Burns
```

Hobomok

I NEVER view the thriving villages of New England, which speak so forcibly to the heart, of happiness and prosperity, without feeling a glow of national pride, as I say, "this is my own, my native land." A long train of associations are connected with her picturesque rivers, as they repose in their peaceful loveliness, the broad and sparkling mirror of the heavens,—and with the cultivated environs of her busy cities, which seem every where blushing into a perfect Eden of fruit and flowers. The remembrance of what we have been, comes rushing on the heart in powerful and happy contrast. In most nations the path of antiquity is shrouded in darkness, rendered more visible by the wild, fantastic light of fable; but with us, the vista of time is luminous to its remotest point. Each succeeding year has left its footsteps distinct upon the soil, and the cold dew of our chilling dawn is still visible beneath the mid–day sun. Two centuries only have elapsed, since our most beautifulvillages reposed in the undisturbed grandeur of nature;—when the scenes now rendered classic by literary associations, or resounding with the din of commerce, echoed nought but the song of the hunter, or the fleet tread of the wild deer. God was here in his holy temple, and the whole earth kept silence before him! But the voice of prayer was soon to be heard in the desert. The sun, which for ages beyond the memory of man had gazed on the strange, fearful worship of the Great Spirit of the wilderness, was soon to shed its splendor upon the altars of the living God. That light, which had arisen amid the darkness of Europe, stretched its long, luminous track across the Atlantic, till the summits of the western world became tinged with its brightness. During many long, long ages of gloom and corruption, it seemed as if the pure flame of religion was every where quenched in blood;—but the watchful vestal had kept the sacred flame still burning deeply and fervently. Men, stern and unyielding, brought it hither in their own bosom, and amid desolation and poverty they kindled it on the shrine of Jevovah. In this enlightened and liberal age, it is perhaps too fashionable to look back upon those early sufferers in the cause of the Reformation, as a band of dark, discontented bigots. Without doubt, there were many broad, deep shadows in their characters, but there was likewise bold and powerful light. The peculiarities of their situation occasioned most of their faults, and atoned for them. They were struck off from a learned, opulent, and powerful nation, under circumstances which goaded and lacerated them almost to ferocity;—and it is no wonder that men who fled from oppression in their own country, to all the hardships of a remote and dreary province, should have exhibited a deep mixture of exclusive, bitter, and morose passions. To us indeed, most ofthe points for which they so strenuously contended, must appear exceedingly absurd and trifling; and we cannot forbear a smile that vigorous and cultivated minds should have looked upon the signing of the cross with so much horror and detestation. But the heart pays involuntary tribute to conscientious, persevering fortitude, in what cause soever it may be displayed. At this impartial period we view the sound policy and unwearied zeal with which the Jesuits endeavored to rebuild their decaying church, with almost as much admiration as we do the noble spirit of reaction which it produced. Whatever merit may be attached to the cause of our forefathers, the mighty effort which they made for its support is truly wonderful; and whatever might have been their defects, they certainly possessed excellencies, which peculiarly fitted them for a van–guard in the proud and rapid march of freedom. The bold outlines of their character alone remain to us. The varying tints of domestic detail are already concealed by the ivy which clusters around the tablets of our recent history. Some of these have lately been unfolded in an old, worn–out manuscript, which accidentally came in my way. It was written by one of my ancestors who fled with the persecuted nonconformists from the Isle of Wight, and about the middle of June, 1629, arrived at Naumkeak on the eastern shore of Massachusetts. Every one acquainted with our early history remembers the wretched state in which they found the scanty remnant of their brethren at that place. I shall, therefore, pass over the young man's dreary account of sickness and distress, and shall likewise take the liberty of substituting my own expressions for his antiquated and almost unintelligible style.

"After a long and wearisome voyage," says he, "we gladly welcomed the peninsula of Shawmut, which, as it lay stretched out in the distance, proclaimed the vicinity of Naumkeak. But the winds seemed resolved to show the full extent of their tantalizing power. All the livelong day we watched the sails as they fluttered loosely round the mast, and listened to the hoarse creaking of the shrouds. Evening at length came on in her softened beauty; and I shall never forget the crowd of sensations which it brought upon my mind. I was in a new world, whose almost unlimited extent lay in the darkness of ignorance and desolation. Earth, sea, and air, seemed in a profound slumber,— and not even the dash of the oar broke in upon their silence. A confusion of thoughts came over my mind, till I was lost and bewildered in their immensity. The scene around me owed nothing of its unadorned beauty to the power of man. He had rarely been upon these waves, and the records of his boasted art were not found in these deserts. I viewed myself as a drop in the vast ocean of existence, and shrunk from the contemplation of human nothingness. Thoughts like these flitted through my mind, till they were lost in dreaming indistinctness. The glittering forehead of the sun was just visible above the waves when I awoke. The wind being fair, the sails were soon spread, and our vessel passed through the waters with a rapid and exhilarating motion. Various accounts had reached us with regard to the New England plantations. The friends of the London company had represented it as a second Canaan; while Mr. Lyford, and other discontented members of the Plymouth church, spoke of it as bleak and sterile,—the scene of tumultuous faction, and domineering zeal. During our voyage I had endeavored to balance these contradictory reports, and to prepare my mind for whatever the result might be; but my philosophy nearly forsook me when I saw our captain point to six miserablehovels, and proclaim that they constituted the whole settlement of Naumkeak. The scene altogether was far worse than my imagination had ever conceived. Among those who came down to the shore to meet us, there were but one or two who seemed like Englishmen. The remainder, sickly and half starved, presented a pitiful contrast to the vigorous and wondering savages who stood among them. I dashed a tear from my eye as the remembrance of England came before me, and jumping upon the beach, I eagerly sought out my old acquaintance, Mr. Conant. He gave me a cordial welcome; but after the numerous greetings had passed, as I slowly walked by his side, I thought his once cheerful countenance had assumed an unusual expression of harshness. He had indeed met with much to depress his native buoyancy of heart. In his younger days he had aspired to the hand of a wealthy and noble lady. Young, volatile, and beautiful, at an age when life seemed all cloudless before her, she left the magnificent halls of her father, and incurred his lasting displeasure by uniting her fortunes with her humble lover. Years rolled on, and misfortune and poverty became their lot. Frustrated in his plans, thwarted by his rivals, misanthropy and gloom sunk deep down into the soul of the disappointed man. It was then the spirit of God moved on the dark, troubled waters of his mind. The stream of life gushed from the fountain within him; but it received the tinge of the dark, turbid soil, through which it passed; and its clear, silent course became noisy amid the eddies of human pride. One by one all the associations connected with the religion of his fathers, were rent away, till kneeling became an abomination, and the prayers of his church a loathing. The arm of royal authority then held a firm grasp on the consciences of men, and England was noplace for him who spoke against the religion of his king. So their children were called together, and the gay young beauty who had sparkled awhile in the court of king James, slept in a rude shelter on a foreign soil. Two boys, the pride of their father's heart, had fallen victims to sickness and famine; and their youngest little blooming fairy had been lately recalled from the home which her grandfather's pity had offered, to watch the declining health of her mother. But the love of woman endured through many a scene of privation and hardship, even after the character of its object was totally changed; and the rigid Calvinist, in that lone place, surrounded by his lovely family, seemed like some proud magnolia of the south, scathed and bared of its leaves, adorned with the golden flowers of the twining jessamine.

Hobomok

"Breakfast was on the board when I first entered, and after the usual salutations had passed, I with several of my companions, sat down to partake of it. It consisted only of roasted pumpkin, a plentiful supply of clams, and coarse cakes made of pounded maize. But unpalatable as it proved, even to me, it was cheerfully partaken by the noble inmates of that miserable hut. As for Mary, her eye sparkled as brightly, and the rich tones of her voice were as merry, as they could have been when her little aerial foot danced along the marble saloon of her grandfather. My eye rested on her, with a painful mixture of sadness and admiration, as in rapid succession she inquired about the scenes of her youth. Even the rough sailors, who were with me, softened their rude tones of voice, and paid to gentleness and beauty the involuntary tribute of respect. Whether the father felt any uneasiness as to the effect of this silent flattery on the young heart of his daughter, or whether habitual asperity had triumphed over natural affectionI know not; but he replied in an angry tone, "Wherefore, Mary, do you ask about those, who bow the knee to Baal, and utter the mummery of common prayer? Methinks it is enough that the hawk has already brought hither a sprig from their tree of corruption, wherewithal to beguile your silly heart."

A blush, which seemed to partake of something more unpleasant than mere embarrassment, passed over the face of the maiden as she answered, "It surely is not strange that I should think often of places where I have enjoyed so much, and should now be tempted to ask questions concerning them, of those who have knowledge thereof."

"Aye, aye," replied the stern old man, "encamped as you are in Elim, beside palm–trees and fountains, you are no doubt looking back for the flesh–pots of Egypt. You'd be willing enough to leave the little heritage which God has planted here, in order to vamp up your frail carcase in French frippery. But I would have you beware, young damsel. Wot ye not that the idle follower of Morton, who was drowned in yonder bay, was inwardly given to the vain forms of the church of England?—and know ye not, that was the reason his God left him, and Satan became his convoy?"

His voice grew louder towards the close, and I saw Mrs. Conant lay her hand upon his, with a beseeching look. Her husband understood the meaning, for he smiled half reluctantly, and rejoined in a subdued tone, "You know it is enough to provoke any body who has a conscience." I was at the time surprised at his sudden change of manner; but during the whole of my intercourse with him afterwards, I noticed that a spirit of tenderness toward his sick wife had survived the wreck of all his kindest feelings. It was indeed but oil upon the surface. The streampursued its own course, and a moment after it would boil and fret at every obstruction. Willing to change the current of his thoughts, I asked whether he had tobacco.

"No," replied he; "but I believe neighbour Oldham hath some; and I will straightway send to him. But by the way, I have been thinking you'd bring us a stock. To my mind, among all king James' blunders with regard to his colonies, (and they were many, God rest his soul,) he never committed a greater, than that of discountenancing the culture of the 'base weed tobacco.' "

"We have a little on board," answered I, "but we have especial orders to see that none be planted in the colony, unless it be some small quantity for mere necessity, and for physic to preserve health, and that is to be partaken by ancient men, and none other."

My friend looked as if he disliked such tokens of restraint. He even went so far as to whisper in my ear, that the "colonies would never do well as long as their prosperity could be hindered by their papistical step–mother from the court of France; and that to be uxorious was a very virtuous vice among common folks, but a very vicious and impolitic virtue in a king."

There were several sailors present who were soon to return to the mother country, and there was little safety in speaking aloud of the king's blind and foolish passion for his Romish queen. So I was fain to speak of the good wishes of my sovereign, and to lament their decrease of numbers, and their late dissatisfaction with the Plymouth elders.

"I have little to say about our troubles," replied Mr. Conant; "but as for numbers, the besom of disease and famine hath been among us, and we are now as an olive tree 'with two or three berries in the top of the uppermost bough, four or five in the outmost fruitful branches thereof.' The Lord's will be done. He hath begun his work, and he will finish it. But it grieveth me to see the strange slips which are set upon our pleasant plants; and when I think thereof, I marvel not that they wither."

"I have heard that Mr. Brown and his brother have been among you some weeks," said I,—"forasmuch as they are staunch Episcopalians, you may refer to them."

"Whom should I mean," rejoined he, "but the two men who like Nabab and Abihu have offered strange incense to the Lord, which he commanded them not? Verily, in due time he will send forth his fire and destroy them from the face of the earth."

As I saw the tears start in Mary's eyes, I felt a vague suspicion that the conversation was, in some way or other, painful to her; and I perceived that the entrance of Mr. Oldham with his tobacco was a relief to her.

"Ah," said the jocular old man, "it's a discrepant way of doing business, to put a neighbour's paw into the fire, instead of helping one's self. Here's Good–man Conant would fain have a fair name on 'tother side the water; but after all, he hath much likeness to Rachel of old, only he keepeth the images in another's tent. But come, let's fill a pipe and talk of byepast times."

All that I could relate concerning our godly brethren in Europe, was amply repaid by Mr. Oldham's humorous description of his own wanderings, mistakes, and sufferings. I had heard that he would speak of his own disgraces with the most shameless effrontery, and laugh at them more loudly than any other man; and I knew that many pious men had doubted the vitalityof his religion, and had felt themselves darkened by intercourse with him;—but although I was shocked at the blasphemous lightness of his speech, I could hardly refrain from countenancing his ludicrous expressions and gestures by a smile.

"I can give you no idea of that guantlet at Plymouth," said he, "when I passed through a band as long as the laws of the Levites, and every man gave me a tug with the butt of his musket. But after all you may think, it was a season of comfortable outpouring. Two passages of Scripture came to my mind, and I was gifted with great light thereupon. David hath it, 'By thee have I passed through a troop;'—and Amos speaketh at a time when, 'If a man fled from a lion, a bear met him; and if he laid his hand upon the wall, a serpent bit him.' Well, it was much the same with me: but as I told you, it was a time of great light, though it was nothing like the first dawning. I'll tell you how that was. I was sitting thus, with my mug of flip before me, and one hand upon each knee, looking straight into the fire, when suddenly I bethought that I was like that smoking brand, with none to pluck it from the burning. So I took a draught of the good stuff, and all at once a light streamed around me, ten times brighter than the earl of Warwick's big lamp."

Hobomok

"Hush," said Mr. Conant. "I cannot have you profane the mysteries of godliness after this fashion. You may mean well,—God grant that you say it not in a spirit of devilish mirth, but forasmuch as you are in my house, I would beg of you to forbear such discourse."

I willingly omit the altercation which followed, which is given at full length in the manuscript; and I likewise pass over the detailed business of the day, such as the unlading of vessels, the delivery of letters, and lastly the theological discussions of the evening.

After much holy and edifying discourse, continues the narration, the family had all retired to rest. But notwithstanding the fatigues of the day, my conflicting feelings would not suffer me to sleep. At length, wearied with the effort, I arose from the bed of straw, and cautiously lifting the wooden latch, I stepped into the open air. As I stood gazing on the reflection of the moon, which reposed in broken radiance on the bay beyond, I tried to think soberly of the difficulties to which I and my oppressed brethren were exposed, and to decide how far I could conscientiously purchase peace and prosperity by conforming to mummeries which my soul detested. Human weakness prompted me to return, and again, when I had most decidedly concluded to stay in New England, the childish witchery of Mary Conant would pass before me, and I felt that the balance was weighed down by earthly motives. I looked out upon the surrounding scenery, and its purity and stillness were a reproach upon my inward warfare. The little cleared spot upon which I was placed, was every where surrounded by dark forests, through which the distant water was here and there gleaming, like the fitful flashes of reason in a disordered mind; and the trees stood forth in all the beauty of that month which the Indians call the "moon of flowers." By degrees the tranquil beauty of the scene, and the mysterious effect of the heavenly host performing their silent march in the far–off wilderness of light, called up the spirit of devotion within me;—and at that moment, forgetful of forms, I knelt to pray that my heart might be kept from the snares of the world.

A shadow was for one moment cast across the bright moonlight; and a slender figure flitted by thecorner of the house. All that I had heard of visitants from other worlds fell coldly on my heart. For a while, I was afraid to ascertain the cause of my fear; but after the person had proceeded a few hesitating steps, she paused and looked back, as if apprehensive of danger. The rays of the full moon rested on her face, and I at once perceived that it was Mary Conant. Had my first fears been realized, I know not that I should have felt more surprise. Among all my conjectures, I could not possibly imagine for what purpose she could be making an excursion at that lonely hour of the night. I remembered the hint, which her father had given, concerning the beguilement of her silly heart, and I could not but suspect that this walk was, in some way or other, connected with the young Episcopalian. Whatever was her project, she seemed half fearful of performing it; for she cast a keen, searching glance behind, and a long, fearful look, at the woods beneath, before she plunged into the thicket. After a moment's consideration, I resolved to follow her, and stepping from behind the tree which had afforded me concealment, I cautiously proceeded along the path which she had taken. She had stopped near a small brook, and when I first discovered her, she had stooped beside it, and taking a knife from her pocket, she opened a vein in her little arm, and dipping a feather in the blood, wrote something on a piece of white cloth, which was spread before her. She rose with a face pale as marble, and looking round timidly, she muttered a few words too low to meet my ear; then taking a stick and marking out a large circle on the margin of the stream, she stept into the magic ring, walked round three times with measured tread, then carefully retraced her steps backward, speaking all the while in a distinct but trembling voice. The following were the only words I could hear,

Whoever's to claim a husband's power,

Come to me in the moonlight hour.

And again,—

Whoe'er my bridegroom is to be,

Step in the circle after me.

She looked round anxiously as she completed the ceremony; and I almost echoed her involuntary shriek of terror, when I saw a young Indian spring forward into the centre.

"What for makes you afraid of Hobomok," said the savage, who seemed scarcely less surprised than herself.

"Wherefore did you come hither," replied the maiden, after the tones of his voice had convinced her that he was real flesh and blood.

"Hobomok much late has been out to watch the deer tracks," answered the Indian; "and he came through the hollow, that he might make the Manitto Asseinah* green as the oak tree."

As he spoke this he threw a large bough upon the heap of rocks to which he had pointed, and looking up to the moon, he uttered something in the Indian tongue, which seemed like a short incantation or prayer. Just as he turned to follow Mary, who was retreating from the woods, a third person made his appearance, in whom I thought I recognized young Brown, specified by Mr. Conant as the strange slip on their pleasant plants. Mary eagerly caught his arm, and seemed glad amid her terror and agitation, to seek the shelter of his offered protection. A fewfriendly words of recognition passed between him and the savage, and the young couple proceeded homewards. A mixed feeling of diffidence and delicacy, had induced me to remain concealed from Mary while I watched over her safety; and the same feeling prompted me to continue where I was until she and her favoured lover were far out of sight and hearing. Hobomok looked after them with a mournful expression of countenance, as he said, "Wonder what for be here alone when the moon gone far away toward the Iroquois. What for sqaw no love like white woman." He stood silent for a short time, and then, taking a large knife from his belt, he cut down two young boughs from the adjoining trees, and threw them, one after another, on the sacrifice heap of his God, as he muttered, "Three times much winnit Abbamocho* said; three times me do."

It seemed but an instant after, that the sound of his heavy tread was lost in the distance.

CHAP. II.

```
In court or hamlet, hut or grove,
Where woman is, there still is love.
Whate'er their nation, form, or feature,
Woman's the same provoking creature.
     — —M. S.
```

A letter from Governor Craddock to Governor Endicott, which had reached them the April before, had given them timely notice of the intended recruits; in which were the following orders. "The desire of the London Company is that you doe endeavour to gettconvenient houseings for the cattell against they doe come; and withal we doe desire whatever bever or fishe can be gotten readie. There hath nott bine a tyme for sale of tymber, these twoe seven years, like unto the present; therefore pittie the shipps should come backe emptye. I wish alsoe that there bee some sassafras and sassaparilla sent us, alsoe goode store of shoemacke, silke grasse, and aught else that may bee useful for dyinge or physicke."

To comply with these various orders, necessarily produced a good deal of hurry and bustle in the infant settlement; and for a long while the sound of the axe was busy and strong among them. And when at length the expected vessels did arrive, and their fine flock of horses, cows, sheep, and goats were well provided for, there was still enough to employ the kind–hearted and healthy, in administering comfort and support to those who had landed among them, weary and sick unto death. My ancestor had already witnessed many of his companions depart this life, exulting that though they were absent from kindred and friends, they were going far beyond the power and cruelty of prelates. Wearied with the wretchedness of the scene, on the 28th of June he departed from Naumkeak, which had now taken the name of Salem, in memory of the peaceful asylum which it it afforded the fugitives. Whether the suspicion of Mary's attachment had any thing to do with the old bachelor's final arrangements, he saith not; but when he again visited America, although he brought a young wife with him, I find he has not failed to speak of her wayward fate with frequent and deep–toned interest.

These brief and scattered hints have now become almost illegible from their age and uncouth spelling, and it was with difficulty I extracted from them materials for the following story.—In a situation soremote, and circumscribed, it may well be supposed that the arrival or departure of a vessel was considered as an affair of great importance, and felt through every fibre of the community. On the occasion I have just referred to, most of the white people from the neighbouring settlements had collected on the beach, together with an almost equal number of the dark children of the forest. Mary had sprung upon a jutting rock, and her sylph–like figure afforded a fine contrast to the decaying elegance of her mother, who was leaning on her arm, the cheerful countenance of Mr. Oldham's buxom daughter, and the tall, athletic form of Hobomok, who stood by her side, resting his healthy cheek upon the hand which supported his bow. By them, and all the motley group around them, the departure of the English vessel was viewed with keen, though varied emotion. The uniform gloom of Mr. Conant's countenance received for one moment a deeper tinge. It was but a passing shadow of human weakness, quickly succeeded by a flush of conscious exultation. His wife, who had left a path all blooming with roses and verdure, and cheerfully followed his rugged and solitary track, pressed back the ready tears, as the remembrance of England came hurrying on her heart. Mary's eyes overflowed with the intense, unrestained gush of youthful feeling. But amid all the painful associations of that moment, the deep interest displayed by my ancestor did not pass unnoticed; and surely the vanity which prompted a lingering look of kindness, might be forgiven, in one growing up in almost unheeded loveliness. "Farewell," said she, as she placed a letter in his hand. "Give this to my grandfather; and many, many kind wishes to good old England."

"Yes," interrupted her father, "many kind wishes to the godly remnant who are among them. Andsince Naumkeak has become old enough to receive a christian name, say ye to them that 'in Salem is his tabernacle, and his dwelling–place in Zion. Here he will break the arrows of the bow, the shield, the sword, and the battle.' But to them who are yet given to the pride of prelacy, and the abomination of common prayer, and likewise to them who are weather–waft up and down with every eddying wind of every new doctrine, say ye to them, that their damnation sleepeth not, and the mist of darkness is reserved for them forever, being of old ordained to condemnation."

This speech was fiercely answered by a dark, lowering looking savage, who stood among the crowd.

"That is Corbitant," said Mary,—"What is it that he says?"

"Your father say Indian arrow be broken at Naumkeak," replied Hobomok,—"Corbitant say the feather be first red with white man's blood."

He would have added more, but the vessels were now sweeping past the rock on which they stood, and every eye was fixed on their motion. Many a hearty salutation, and blunt compliment were paid to Sally Oldham, and many a hat was waved in respectful adieu to Mrs. Conant and her daughter. The loud response which the sailors gave to the kind farewells of their friends on shore, was soon lost in the distance, and one by one the people slowly dispersed. Mrs. Conant took the arm of her husband, and Mary lingered far behind, in hopes of obtaining a conference with Sally Oldham. But one Mr. Thomas Graves seemed to have been deeply smitten with the comely countenance of the latter damsel; and never for a moment doubting that the fascination was reciprocal, he became somewhat obtrusively officious. It was singular to observe the difference of deportment

14

betweenhim and the Indian. Whenever Hobomok gazed upon Mary, it was with an expression in which reverence was strikingly predominant. And now, with more than his usual taciturnity, he walked at a short distance before them, and eagerly pointed with his bow, when it was necessary to obviate any little difficulties in their path. But he from the Isle of Wight, seemed resolved that one of the young ladies should be aware of the presence of a noisy admirer, and with abundance of stammering awkwardness, he began, "You are Mr. Oldham's daughter, I think?"

"I have been told so, sir," replied the mischievous girl.

"The world is dark and dismal enough in any place," continued the man of a wo–begone countenance,—"more especially when we think of the regiments of sin which are marching up and down in its borders; but I should think it would be ten times darker to a well–favored young woman, here in this wilderness."

"If you mean me," answered the maiden, "I pass my time merry enough, in the long run; but there is no danger of our forgetting the dolors while we have your visage amongst us."

"I sha'nt be called to give an account of my looks," replied the offended suitor, "inasmuch as God made them in such form and likeness as pleased him. But I perceive you have no savor of goldliness about you, and are clean carried away by the crackling thorns of worldly mirth."

"My friend is like Rachel of old," interrupted her smiling companion. "She feedeth her cattle and draweth them water, and waiteth for some Jacob to journey hither."

"And what would you say, damsel, if he were at your very door," rejoined Mr. Graves, with an uncouthdistension of his jaws, which was doubtless meant for one of love's gentle, insinuating smiles. "And when Jacob knew Rachel he kissed her," continued he, as he courageously put his arm round her neck, to suit his action to the words.

"I have had enough of that from the sanctified Mr. Lyford," said the resolute maiden, as she gave him a blow, which occasioned a sudden and involuntary retreat.

Hobomok

"Well done, Sally," said the hoarse voice of her father, who just then stept from among the trees, half choked with laughter, and for a moment forgetful of the decorum which he usually maintained in her presence. "Why, fellow, thou'rt smitten indeed; but it ill beseemeth thee to put on a rueful face at this disaster. The damsel is not worth the tears, which an onion draweth forth."

Sally gladly left her discomfited lover to recover himself as he could, and bidding a hasty good–morning to Hobomok, as he stood laughing and muttering to himself, she followed Mary, who with an air of girlish confidence had beckoned her into a narrow footpath which led through the woods. For a few moments the girls united in almost convulsive fits of laughter.

"Did you ever see such a fellow?" said Sally. "Every day since they landed, he has been at my elbow, trying to make love by stammering and stuttering about the crackling thorns of worldly mirth; and I verily think he believes that I have been greatly delighted therewith. A plague on all such sanctified looking folks. There was Mr. Lyford, (I don't care if he was a minister) he was always talking about faith and righteousness, and the falling–off of the Plymouth elders, and yet many a sly look and word he'd give me, when his good–woman was out of the way. Imarvel that fools can always find utterance, inasmuch as some men of sense are so dumb."

"Men of sense will speak all in good time, if you will wait patiently," answered Mary. "But you don't know how glad I am that it happened to be your father, instead of mine, who saw you strike Mr. Graves."

"So am I," replied her companion. "Though he is your father, to my thinking he is over fond of keeping folks in a straight jacket; and I'm sure our belt is likely to be buckled tight enough by the great folks there in London. In my poor judgment it is bad enough that we've come over into this wilderness to find elbow room for our consciences, without being told how long a time we may have to stop and breathe in. Every bout I knit in my stocking is to be set down in black and white, and sent over to the London Company forsooth. I suppose by and by the drops we drink and the mouthfuls we eat must be counted, and their number sent thither."

"I am sure," replied Mary, "when you remember how many Indians we have lately met, whom Morton's unthinking wickedness has armed with powder and firelocks, you will be glad that we have three hundred more defenders around us, whatever price we may pay therefor. Indeed Sally, I'm weary of this wilderness life. My heart yearns for England, and had it not been for my good mother, I would gladly have left Naumkeak to–day."

"I can't but admire ye've been content so long, Miss Mary, considering what ye left behind you. If you'd staid there, who knows but you might have been Lady Lincoln? But as for this purlieu of creation, I know of no chance a body has for a husband, without they pick up some stray Narraganset, or wandering Tarateen."

"O, don't name such a thing," said Mary, shuddering.

"Why, what makes you take me in earnest?" answered Sally. "But perhaps since there are so many young folks to pick and choose among, you'll be weary of my crackling mirth, as that stupid Graves calls it."

"No, Sally, these new comers won't make me forget how kind you have always been in sickness and health; but, to tell you the truth, there is something troubles me—and if you'll promise not to tell of it, I'll tell you."

"O, I'll promise that, and keep it too. If I was disposed to tell your secrets, I don't know any body but owls and bats I should tell them too."

"Well then, you must know, the other night I did a wicked thing. It frightens me to think thereof. You know the trick I told you about? Well, a few weeks ago, I tried it; and just as I was saying over the verses the third time, Hobomok, the Indian, jumped into the circle."

"Hobomok, the Indian!"

"Yes;—and I screamed when I saw him."

"I believe so indeed. But was it he, real flesh and blood?"

"It was he himself; though I thought at first, it must be his ghost?"

"But how came he there, at that time of night?"

"That's more than I can tell. He said he came to throw a bow on the sacrifice heap, down in Endicott's hollow; but I don't know what should put it into his head just at that time. What do you suppose did?"

"I'm sure I don't know, Mary. I think it is an awful wicked thing to try these tricks. There's no telling what may come of asking the devil's assistance. He is an acquaintance not so easily shook off, when you've once spoke with him, to my certain knowledge. Myfather says he's no doubt the Lord has given Beelzebub power to choose many a damsel's husband, to recompense her for such like wickedness. I'm sure I have been curious enough to know, but I never dared to speak to Satan about the matter."

"I believe it is a sin to be repented of; but what could I do? Father won't suffer me to see Charles any where, if he can help it; and if I dared to be disobedient to him, I wouldn't do it while my poor mother was alive, for I know it would break her heart. But there are two things more about this affair which puzzle me. Just as I came out of the hollow, I met Charles. He said he dreamed I was in danger there, and he could not help coming to see whether I was there or not. So I told him how foolish I had been, and he laughed, and said he should be my husband after all. But the strangest thing of all, is, that Englishman you saw me give a letter to, to–day, whispered in my ear never to try a trick again, for fear worse should come of it. I wonder how he knew any thing concerning it?"

"Likely as not, he followed you. Or may be Hobomok told him. But I am glad Mr. Brown dreamed about it. After all, I guess he is to be the one; and Hobomok only came that way after some stray fox or squirrel he caught sight of."

"I don't know how it was," replied Mary, with a deep sigh. "I suppose I must submit to whatever is fore–ordained for me. Folks who have the least to do with love are the best off. The longer you keep as free from it as you are now, the happier you"ll be."

"May be you don't know how free that is," rejoined Sally. "If you had half an eye for other folks' affairs, you would remember something about a young man in Plymouth who used to help me milk my cows, inasmuch as you have often heard me speak of him.Do you know I spoke to him on the beach this morning? I should have had a good opportunity to have seen him again, if it had not been for that everlasting fellow, talking about 'crackling thorns;' I would not care an'he had one of them in his tongue. Howsomever, if I guess right concerning Mr. Collier, he did'nt come up to see the cattle.

But I can't stop to say any more, for the cows an't milked yet; and now these new orders have come from London, and there are so many sick folks from the vessels, we shall have enough to do. So, good bye," said the roguish damsel, as she sprung over the log inclosure, into her father's farm–yard.

CHAP. III.

        I would not wish
Any companion in the world but you;
Nor can imagination form a shape,
Beside yourself, to like of.
    — Tempest

Notwithstanding her increase of avocations, and the many wearisome nights she had spent in tending the sick who had come among them, there was no one more heartily rejoiced at the new order of things than Sally Oldham, whom I find mentioned in the manuscript as "a promp and jolly damsell, much given to lightnesse of speeche, but withal virtuous." The merry maiden, amid all the labours and privations necessarily attendant upon their lonely situation at Plymouth, had found means to put on the airs of rustic coquetry with considerable success; and therefore she had felt no little regret when her father's passionateand unjustifiable conduct toward the ruling elders, had subjected him to the shameful punishment referred to in the first chapter, and driven his family from their comparatively comfortable home. Her only consolation during this period was in recounting to Mary the numerous acts of gallantry she had received from her Plymouth lovers. The young man whom she had seen upon the beach, on the morning of the 28th, had a kinder remembrance than all his competitors; and when she heard that he had walked from Plymouth, with Hobomok for his guide, in the true spirit of female vanity, she judged that nothing but her own pretty face was the object of his journey. Still it seemed she had some fears about his diffidence, for when she had taken her milking–pail and quietly seated herself beside the miserable pile of logs and boughs, which she dignified with the name of a cow–house, she muttered to herself, "I wish Collier was a little easier to take a hint." Her cogitations were interrupted by a well known voice, which had become associated in Sally's mind with nought but "the crackling of thorns." "What brought you hither, Mr. Graves?" inquired the maiden.

"I thought," replied he, as he stood scratching his head with one hand, and holding out the other in token of amity, "I thought, may be, you'd repent your rashness this morning, inasmuch as husbands don't grow on every tree in these deserts."

Notwithstanding this cogent argument, well backed with humble gestures, the offered peace was rejected; and his clammy hand remained awkwardly upraised in the air, like the quivering claw of a dying lobster.

"I tell you sir," rejoined the angry damsel, "that I am weary of your unsavory discourse; and if husbands like you, grew by hundreds on the lowest boughs of the trees, they might stay there till doomsday before I'd stop to pluck 'em therefrom."

"But you'll let me take the milk across for you," continued the persevering suitor, as she stept upon a narrow board that was laid across a deep ditch. Sally, in the wickedness of her heart, held out the pail to him; but just as he was in the act of taking it, she managed by a gentle motion, to place him ancle–deep in the mud below; then turning round for an instant, with a loud and provoking laugh, she soon disappeared.

As Mr. Graves rose, and struck off the mud from his clothes, he murmured, "It is plain she is given over to a reprobate mind;" and it was noticed he never afterwards darkened Mr. Oldham's dwelling.

To Sally the day seemed to pass tardily away, for she had predicted, that the evening would bring a visit from Mr. Collier; and accordingly the manuscript states, that "the curtains of nighte were but halfe shut, when he seated himselfe beside Mr. Oldham, who was turning down many a dropp of the bottell, and burning tobacco with all the ease he could, discoursing between whiles of the dolorous beginning of the settlement, when their cups of beer ran as small as water in a sandie landie, and they were forced to lengthene out their own foode with acorns; and anon talking of the greate progress they would make with their fellowe labourers, now the summer sun had changed the earth's white–furred gowne into a green mantell."

"I must say," observed the young man, "that it is a bosom–breaking thing to me, when I think the gulf atween us and old England is too wide to leap over with a lope–staff. I am the last who would put my hand to the plough, and then look back; but I must say, could I have cast up, in the beginning, what this wilderness work would have cost us, I should have been staggered much, and very hardly have set sail."

Hobomok

"Why, to my thinking, Mr. Collier," replied Oldham, "England is no place now–a–days for christian folks to live within. They talk about their reformed church, but I tell you their bishops, their deans, and their deacons, are all whelps from the Roman litter; and tame 'em as you can, the nature of the beast will shew itself. It is a sad pity that king Charles (I mean no disrespect to his majesty) should suffer those black coats from the ninneversities to get upon his royal back—I trow they'll ride him to destruction. But, as I was saying, England is full of malignant enemies to the true faith; and after all, a body can as pithily practise the two great precepts of the gospel in this, as well as in any other place; which precepts I take to be mortification and sanctification."

"Nobody can doubt there is room enough to practise the first, father," interrupted Sally, who had all along been quietly knitting in the corner, and who had begun to be weary of such sober discourse.

"You talk like a prating ideot, as you are," replied her father, furiously. "What with your own hankering after French gew–gaws, and the grand stories of your Moabitish companion, you have your head clean turned from sound sense and sober godliness."

"You know, Goodman," rejoined his wife, "that howsomever gracious and obedient our children may be, there have been no small hardships during our sojourning here, both for their young hearts and limbs too. Besides, Sally is included in the covenant with her parents, and to my mind, no member of Christ's body should be wrested from his church by harsh words."

"You utter the sayings of a foolish woman," answered her angry spouse. "I'm far from being clear whether the covenant we entered into is binding. Them ruling elders there at Plymouth, brought anabundance of pragmatical zeal, and rigid separation from the Netherlands. They've clapped a vizor on their own traditions, and placed them cheek–by–jowl with revealed truth; and many an honest man will be puzzled to distinguish 'em therefrom. And still more am I in the dark whether this stray imp, laughing with every idle fellow she meets, (the better for her that she meets few of them)"—Just at that moment, recollecting the discomfiture of Mr. Graves, his natural propensity to fun overcame his resentment, and he placed both his hands upon his sides, and burst into a broad laugh. The look of surprise which his wife and Mr. Collier glanced towards him, and the drollery which was peeping out of the corners of Sally's mouth, recalled him to decorum; and looking towards his daughter with an expression that

21

seemed to say, "You'd no right to understand me," he passed his hand over his face and resumed, "I say, I am much in the dark whether she be implied in the covenant with us. It is not every child of a righteous man who is among the elect; nor is the offspring of the wicked always fore−ordained to damnation. If there be a good child in Jeroboam's family, he is specified; and if there be a cursed Ham among the children of Noah, he hath his brand."

"Well," Goodman Oldham, interrupted his guest, "it is not for us to tell who is among the elect, and who not, forasmuch as we cannot enter into the counsels of the Most High. And surely when the hearts of stout men grow faint in this enterprise, we need not marvel that women, and young women too, should betimes think of their hardships, and complain thereof. Jacob was regardful of the weakness of the women and little ones of his land."

"I'm sure I never murmured when worst came toworst," said Sally, as she glanced an eye of moist gratitude on her kind advocate.

"I tell you," said Mr. Oldham, without noticing her interruption, "you don't know as much about these weaker vessels as I do; and mayhap you feel concerning them as I used to in by−gone times. But I tell you they are the source of every evil that ever came into the world. I don't refer in special manner to that great tree of sin planted by Eve; but I say they are the individual cause of every branch and bud from that day downwards. I charge you enter not into their path, for destruction layeth wait therein."

"You are one of the last men who should say so," answered his companion, as he looked towards his care−worn and uncomplaining wife.

"She is as good as any of her kind, to be sure," said the rigid old man, as he took his tobacco from his mouth, and drank a hearty draught of cider from the stone mug; then replacing his tobacco, and drawing his sleeve across his mouth, he passed the beverage to Mr. Collier, as he said, "It is a long time since I have tasted the like of this. It's as good as was ever tipped over the tongue of king Charles, God help him, and Satan leave off helping the queen and his bishops. I'd fain stay and argue with you a bit, Mr. Collier, inasmuch as I've been told you are falling into some Antinomian notions; but I must go up to Governor Endicott's awhile, to see how the cattle are to be divided atween us; and I must stop to see a few of the poor sick souls about us. So if you want, you can draw more upon the cider, and may be my good woman will give you a bit of bread and cheese. We have plenty of provisions since the ships were sent hither, the Lord be thanked." So saying, the old man tookdown his hat from the wooden peg on which it always hung, and closed the door after him.

"Mr. Oldham is a strange talking man," observed his wife; "but he barks worse than he bites."

"I know his ways," answered Mr. Collier. "It is a pity he strikes fire so quick; but it proveth there is good metal in him. And now, Sally, I have a present for you," continued he, as he placed a letter in her hand, which she received with blushing curiosity, and read as follows:

"Deere Maidene,

"This comes to reminde you of one you sometime knew at Plimouth. One to whome the remembrance of your comely face and gratious behaviour, hath proved a very sweete savour. Many times I have thought to write to you, and straightnesse of time only hath prevented. There is much to doe at this seasone, and wee have reason to rejoyce, though with fier and trembling, that we have wherewithal to worke.

"Forasmuch as it is harde to saye unto a damsell, wilt thou bee my wife? I have chosene the rather to place it upon pure white paper, the embleme of your hearte. Which if you will pleese soe to answer, you will much oblige your dutyfull servante. For as Jacob loved Rachelle, and toyled many yeers for her, so loveth

Your trew freynde, James Hopkins."

Mrs. Oldham, with a slight tincture of the modern policy of mothers, had gone out to "neighbour Conant's," when Sally first began to read the foregoing; and luckily she was not there to witness the vexed and disappointed looks of her daughter.

"I suppose I know the writer," said Mr. Collier, smiling as she laid down the paper, "What answer shall I carry thereto?"

Hobomok

"It is from that screech–owl of a Hopkins, who usedto be forever bawling Old Hundred in my ears," replied the maiden; "and you may say to him that I have much more kindness for his sheep than for him."

"Peradventure you are in sport," said her astonishished visitor. "You'll find few men in this wilderness of more respectability than my good friend Hopkins."

"Well, if he can find a Rachel, assuredly I have no objection to his toiling for her; but if I should be very near her, I should verily whisper in her ear to give him twice a fourteen years' tug."

"So you are really going to break poor James' heart?" inquired her friend, after a moment's pause.

"If so be there is such a thing as a heart in his big carcase of clay," rejoined the maiden, "I'm willing it should be shattered a bit."

"Poor fellow, what will he think of all this?" inquired the young man, thoughtfully.

"There's divers things he might think," answered the damsel, who began to be out of patience with his stupid modesty. "He might think, if he wanted a wife again, that she was worth the trouble of coming after; or peradventure he can send to king James' plantation and buy one, for a hundred pounds of tobacco. Think you that Isaac would have had good speed with the daughter of Bethuel, with all his jewels of silver and gold, if he had sent by so clever a messenger as yourself, John?"

If one might judge from the expression of the young man's face, he did at length begin to have a faint perception of the truth. An awkward silence followed, till Sally, struck with the ludicrous situation of them both, burst into her usual laugh. "I tell you what, Mr. Collier," said she, "to my thinking, you are the stupidest fellow I ever looked upon; and when you set out upon other men's business, I advise youto do it faithfully, but nevertheless to keep an eye upon your own."

The young man rested one hand upon his knee, turned his bright blue eyes and sun–burnt face towards her, and seemed lost in utter bewilderment.

Hobomok

"But,—hem—but what can I do?" said he.

"I know what you can do; but what you will do, is of your own choosing. I have heretofore told you what to say to Hopkins; and I now tell you, John Collier, if you had sent by him, instead of he by you, and my father had said to me, 'wilt thou go unto this man?' I should verily have said, 'I will go.' "

"And I," rejoined the Plymouth messenger, smiling as he rose and laid his hand upon her shoulder, "I would assuredly have come out to meet thee, and bring thee into my tent. But what perplexes me most is, how I am to account for this to my friend Hopkins and the church."

"You may tell James," replied she, "that you was blind, till I would put eyes into your head; and as for the church, it is enough for them to square and clip our consciences without putting a wedge atwixt folk's hearts."

"It is not well to give away to lightness of speech in speaking of the dignities of the church," observed her lover, "though I know well you mean no harm."

What farther passed between the young people, before the return of the family, is not specified in the manuscript; but an asterisk points to the bottom of the page, where it saith that "the matteer was made knowne to her parents, wherewithall they were welle pleased; more especially as they founde he was nott given to the dreadfull herese of the Antinomians."

Mr. and Mrs. Oldham returned shortly, at least it seemed so to those they had left behind. The old man replaced his hat upon its accustomed peg, drewto the fire his large oaken chair, the pride and ornament of his house, and, after a few discontented remarks about the intended division of the cattle, he took down the big Bible from the shelf, which had been nailed up on purpose for its reception, and read in a loud monotonous tone the 9th chapter of Romans. The prayer which followed was in somewhat too harsh and austere a tone for the voice christian entreaty, but in that rude place it was impressive in its solemn simplicity. The family devotions were concluded with the favourite tune of the great Reformer, in which the clear, rich, native melody of the daughter, contrasted finely with the deep, heavy bass of the father. Soon after, Sally and her mother closed the door which separated their humble little apartment from the outer room, leaving Mr. Oldham and his visitor to discourse about the Antinomians, Anabaptists, and sundry other sects, which even at that early period began to trouble the Seceding Church.

CHAP. IV.

```
        Know ye the famous Indian race?
How their light form springs, in strength and grace,
Like the pine on their native mountain side,
That will not bow in its deathless pride;
Whose rugged limbs of stubborn tone,
No plexuous power of art will own,
But bend to Heaven's red bolt alone!
    — Yamoyden
```

Jacob's heart could not have swelled with more exultation, when he journeyed from Padan—aram with his two bands, than was evinced by our forefathers, when they exhibited their newly arrived riches to the wondering natives. As for the poor, unlettered Indians, it exceeded their comprehension how buffaloes, as they termed them, could be led about by the horns, and be compelled to stand or move at the command of men; and they could arrive at no other conclusion than that the English were the favorite children of the Great Spirit, and that he had taught them words to speak to them. To these, and similar impressions, may be ascribed the astonishing influence of the whites over these untutored people. That the various tribes did not rise in their savage majesty, and crush the daring few who had intruded upon their possessions, is indeed a wonderful exemplification of the superiority of intellect over mere brutal force. At the period of which we speak, the thoughtless and dissipated Morton, whom we find mentioned so frequently in our early history, had done much to diminish their reverence for the English. Partly from avarice, and partly from revenge of Governor Endicott's spirited proceedings against his company at Merry Mount, he had sold them rifles, and taught them to take a steady and quick—sighted aim; so that they now boasted they could speak thunder and spit fire as well as the white man. Of late, too, their councils became dark and contentious, for their princes began to fear encroachments upon their dominions, and their prophets were troubled with rumors of a strange God. The Pequods looked with hatred upon the English, as an obstacle to their plan of universal dominion; the Narragansets stood trembling between the increasing power of their new neighbours, and the haughty threats of their enemies; some of the discontented sachems of Mount Haup had broken out in open rebellion; and even the firm faith of Massasoit himself had, at times, been doubted. In such a state of things, embassies and presents were frequently necessary to supportthe staggering friendship of the well disposed tribes. Accordingly, the second day after his arrival from Plymouth, Hobomok proceeded to Saugus, carrying presents from the English, and a message from Massasoit to Sagamore John. At this wigwam he met Corbitant, a stubborn enemy to the Europeans, and all who favored them. He had been among the Pequods of late, and was exasperated beyond measure that he had in vain offered their war–belt (in token of alliance against the English) to Miantonimo, the great sachem of the Narragansets. Possessed of a mind more penetrating, and a temper even more implacable than most of his brethren, his prophetic eye foresaw the destruction of his countrymen, and from his inmost soul he hated the usurpers. Besides, there was a personal hostility between him and Hobomok concerning an affair of love, in which Corbitant thought one of his kindred had been wronged and insulted; and more than once they had sought each other's life. At the moment Hobomok entered, he was engaged in eager conversation with Sagamore John, concerning his connexion with the English, and scarcely was he seated, ere he exclaimed,

"Shame on you, Hobomok! The wolf devours not its own; but Hobomok wears the war–belt of Owanux,* and counts his beaver for the white man's squaw. Oh cursed Owanux! The buffalo will die of the bite of a wasp, and no warrior will pluck out his sting. Oh cursed Owanux! And yet Miantonimo buckles on their war belt, and Massasoit says, their pipe smokes well. Look to the east, where the sun rises among the Taratines; to the west, where he sets among the valiant Pequods: then look to the south, among the cowardly Narragansets,and the tribes of Massasoit, thick as the trees of his forests; then look far to the north, where the Great Spirit lifts his hatchet* high above the head of the Nipnet! And say, are not the red men like the stars in the sky, or the pebbles in the ocean? But a few sleeps more, let Owanux such the blood of the Indian, where be the red man then? Look for yesterday's tide, for last year's blossoms, and the rainbow that has hid itself in the clouds! Look for the flame that has died away, for the ice that's melted, and for the snow that lights on the waterfall! Among them you will find the children of the Great Spirit. Yes, they will soon be as an arrow that is lost in its flight, and as the song of a bird flown by."

This was uttered with a smile of bitter irony, and in a tone so loud and fierce, that every eye was fixed on the speaker. Sagamore John laid down his pipe to listen; his squaw shook her head mournfully as he uttered his predictions; and his sons stood gazing upon Corbitant, till the fire flashed from their young eyes, and their knives were half drawn from the belt. Even Hobomok, whose loves and hates had become identified with the English, admired the eloquence of his enemy, and made a melancholy pause ere he answered, "Corbitant knows well that the arm of Hobomok is not weak, nor his cheek pale in time of battle; but if the quiver of the Narragansets be filled against the Yengees, know you not, that they themselves will be trodden down, like snow, in the warpath of the Pequods?"

"That's the song of the lame bird, to lead from its nest," replied Corbitant, sarcastically. "Would Hobomok weep, if the Pequod should lift his head to theclouds, and plant one foot among the Taratines, and the other far, far away among the Caddoques? Would he utter one groan, if the hatchet of Sassacus were buried deep in the brains of Pokanecket's child? No! and yet Hobomok asked that the child of Pokanecket might be his squaw; but his beaver skins were not brought, and she cooked the deer for Ninigret's son.* Hobomok saves his tears for the white–faced daughter of Conant, and his blood for the arrow of Corbitant, that his kinswoman may be avenged."

Hobomok lifted his tomahawk in wrath, as his adversary uttered these insulting words. "Who dares speak of groans and tears," said he, "to him whose heart has been calm in the fight, and whose eye winked not at the glancing of arrows?"

Corbitant answered by a scornful laugh, and the hatchet would have descended on his head, had not Sagamore John stept between them, as he said, "Listen to the words of an ancient chief. The Great Spirit loves not the sacrifice of young blood, when it is shed in quarrel. Smoke the pipe of peace, my children; and I will tell you of days that are gone by, when the war–whoop of John was heard the loudest among his tribe, and his arrow brought down the deer at her swiftest speed."

To have refused to listen to the stories of an old man would have been contrary to all rules of Indian decorum; but before the fierce, young spirits composed themselves to respectful silence, a challenge of proud looks was exchanged, as Corbitant muttered, "When the big sea–bird up yonder, go back to their great land–chief, king Charles, the white squaw's father, say Indian arrow be broken at Naumkeak. Let him look to't that the wolf be not near his wigwam."

Hours passed away while the young sons sat devouring the words of their father, and even his guests seemed to have forgotten their own hatred, in the eager reverence with which they listened to him. His squaw, in the mean time, had taken her coarse, roasted cakes from the fire, and placed some cold venison before her visitors, and pointed to it with a look of pride, as she said, "The arm of my sanup is old, but you see his arrow is yet swifter than the foot of the deer. May his sons bring him food in his old age."

The hospitable meal was gratefully partaken, and all John's exploits in war and hunting being told, Hobomok, having found means to transact the business for which he came, arose to depart. Corbitant, too, threw his quiver over his shoulder, and tightened his belt, as if preparing for a journey. Sagamore John, laying his hand upon his arm, whispered something in his ear, and he reluctantly resumed his seat. In the height of gratitude for some recent favor, he had promised to obey the old chief in his first request, provided it had no connexion with the English; and now that twenty minutes of his time were asked, he would gladly have given all the animals he ever caught, to be released from his promise. However, his word was unbroken; and Hobomok went forth alone. For a few moments he hesitated whether or not to go back and seek satisfaction for the insults he had received from the kinsman of his once betrothed bride. But he remembered what Corbitant had said about the Indian arrows being broken at Naumkeak, and though he did not exactly understand the import of his words, he well knew that an Indian never spoke thus, without some deep laid plan of vengeance. An undefined apprehension of danger to Mr. Conant's family passed over his heart, and after a few reluctant steps backward, he turned round hastily and walked forward, as he said, "It isn't the love of life,—but if I should be killed in these woods, who will be left to tell her of her danger? 'Twould be pity so young a bird should be brought down in its flight."

As he walked on in a hurried, irregular pace, love, resentment, and wounded pride, were all busy at his heart–strings. He had left Pokanecket's daughter, because he loathed the idea of marriage with her; but he never had thought, and till now he never had been told, that Mary Conant was the cause. Soon after her arrival at Plymouth, Mary had administered cordials to his sick mother, which restored her to life after the most skilful of their priests had pronounced her hopeless; and ever since that time, he had looked upon her with reverence, which almost amounted to adoration. If any dregs of human feeling were mingled with these sentiments, he at least, was not aware of it; and now that the idea was forced upon him, he rejected it, as a kind of blasphemy. With these thoughts were mixed a melancholy presentiment of the destruction of his race, and stern, deep, settled hatred of Corbitant.

29

Hobomok

As he came in sight of the seacoast, the sun was just setting behind the ledge of rocks which stretched along to his right; and the broad blue harbour of Salem lay full in his view, as tranquil as the slumbers of a young heart devoid of crime. The spring birds were warbling among the trees, or floating along so lightly, that they scarcely dipped their wing in the still surface of the water. There was something in the unruffled aspect of things, which tended to soothe the turbulence of human passion. By degrees the insults of Corbitant, the remembrance of Pokanecket's child, the clouds which imagination had seen lowering over the fate of his nation, and even the dangerof his English friends, became more dim and fleeting; till at length, the spirit of devotion sat brooding over the soul of the savage. The star, which had arisen in Bethlehem, had never gleamed along his path; and the dark valley of the shadow of death had never been illuminated with the brightness of revealed truth. But though the intellect be darkened, there are rays from God's own throne, which enter into the peacefulness and purity of the affections, shedding their mild lustre on the ignorance of man.

Philosophy had never held up her shield against the sun, and then placed her dim taper in his hand, while she pointed to the "mundane soul," in which all human beings lost their identity; nor had he ever read of that city "whose streets were of gold, and her gates of pearl, in the light of which walked the nations of them which were saved;" but there was within him a voice loud and distinct, which spoke to him of another world, where he should think, feel, love, even as he did now. He had never read of God, but he had heard his chariot wheels in the distant thunder, and seen his drapery in the clouds. In moods like these, thoughts which he could not grasp, would pass before him, and he would pause to wonder what they were, and whence they came. It was with such feelings that he stopped, and resting his head againt a large hemlock, which lifted its proud branches high above the neighboring pines, he gazed on the stars, just visible above the horizon. He stood thus some moments, when a rustling sound broke in upon the stillness, and an arrow whizzed past him, and caught in the corner of his blanket. He turned round suddenly, and saw Corbitant advancing towards him with an uplifted hatchet.

"Ha! said he, with his accustomed laugh of scorn, I thought Hobomok winked not at the glancing of arrows. When did Corbitant flee to the woods, to save life, when he had been dared to the fight?"

Few words passed between them, and desperate was the struggle which ensued. For awhile it seemed doubtful who would get the victory, amid the fierceness of their savage

30

warfare; till at length a violent blow on the temple laid Corbitant senseless on the ground.

"Love your enemy," was a maxim Hobomok had never learned, and the tomahawk was already raised above the head of his stupified victim, when the sound of voices was heard in the thicket, and springing into his former path, he pursued his way homeward, as fleetly as some wild animal of the forest. A few moments brought in view the settlement of Salem; and amid the lights, which here and there twinkled indistinctly through the trees, he quickly distinguished the dwelling of Mary Conant.

CHAP. V.

```
The light within enthusiasts, who let fly
Against our pen-and-ink divinity;
Who boldly do pretend, (but who'll believe it?)
If Genesis were lost they could retrieve it.
    — Nicholas Noyles
```

During their solitary stay at Naumkeak, wasted as the young colony had been with sickness, famine, and fearful apprehension, the buoyant spirits and kind heart of Sally Oldham, had proved an almost solitary source of enjoyment to Mary Conant. True, there were few points of congeniality either in native character, or habitual tendency of mind. The noblerprinciples of the soul may long remain latent amid the depressing atmosphere of circumstance and situation; but the rich-toned instrument needs but a skillful hand to produce the finest combinations of harmony, and even to the rude touch of the winds, it will occasionally yield its sweet response of wayward melody. Indeed it seemed as if the chilling storms, which had lowered over the young life of Mary Conant, had not only served to call forth the fervid hues of feeling in their full perfection, but had likewise strengthened her native elegance of mind. The intellectual, like the natural sun, sheds its own bright and beautiful lustre on the surrounding gloom, till every object on which it shines seems glowing into life; and amid all the dreariness of poverty, and the weight of affliction (the heavier, that it was borne far from the knowledge and sympathy of the world), Mary found much to excite her native fervor of imagination. The stars were there, in their silent, sparkling beauty, and the fair-browed moon smiled on the hushed, still loveliness of nature. The monarch of day paused ere he gathered around him his brilliant drapery of clouds, and gazed on these wild dominions with as much pride as upon fairer and warmer climes. But all associations of this nature formed a "sanctum sanctorum" in the recesses of Mary's heart, and Sally Oldham was one of the last to penetrate it. She thought nothing of the stars but of their luckly or unlucky influences, viewed the moon as a well-favored planet, that had much to do with the weather, and saw nothing in the setting sun but a hint to do her out-door work. But whether the understanding finds reciprocation or not, the heart must have sympathy; and amid the depression of spirits, naturally induced by the declining health of her mother, and the disheartening influence of the stern, dark circle in which she moved, Mary found awelcome relief in unlocking all her hopes, fears, and disappointments to her untutored friend. Her usual placid state of feeling had been restored by the ample confession she had made concerning an action, which she more than half feared would call down the vengeance of Heaven upon her; and when Hobomok entered the room, after the excursion mentioned in the last chapter, she was quietly seated amid the circle, which had assembled at her father's house. It was indeed a scene of varied character. The mother and daughter, as we have already observed, possessed that indefinable outline of elegance, which is seldom entirely effaced from those of high birth and delicate education. In immediate contrast were the stern, hard features of Mr. Conant, and the singular countenance of Mr. Oldham, which reminded one of gleams of light through a grated window, for the deep furrows of passion, and the shadows of worldly disappointment, were in vain cast over its natural drollery of expression. Then there was the fine, bold expression of Governor Endicott, and the dolorous visage of Mr. Graves, which seemed constantly to say, "the earth is a tomb and man a fleeting vapour;' and lastly the manly beauty of Hobomok, as he sat before the fire, the flickering and uncertain light of a few decaying embers falling full upon his face. This Indian was indeed cast in nature's noblest mould. He was one of the finest specimens of elastic, vigorous elegance of proportion, to be found among his tribe. His long residence with the white inhabitants of Plymouth had changed his natural fierceness of manner into haughty, dignified reserve; and even that seemed softened as his dark, expressive eye rested on Conant's daughter.

"We have heard somewhat of an alliance between the Pequods and Narragansets," said Governor Endicott, as Hobomok seated himself. "What says Sagamore John concerning this matter?"

"He said it was a cloud gone by," was the laconic answer.

"And do you think the Pequods will ever prevail on them to join against us, Hobomok?"

Hobomok

"The quivers of the Pequod is full of arrows," replied the Indian; "his belt is the skin of a snake, and he suffers no grass to grow upon his war–path. He needs not the sinew of the Narraganset to draw the arrow to the head."

"When you were among the Narragansets what was their speech thereupon?" inquired the chief magistrate.

"Miantonimo called king Charles his good English father," answered Hobomok. "He wore not the belt of the Pequod, and his sachems smoked not the pipe of Sassacus. But that was a few sleeps ago. A man may tell the changes of the moon, but it is not so with the word of a Narraganset."

He rose as he said this, and stood for some moments at the aperture which admitted the light, gazing intently on the surrounding woods; but if there was any thing like anxiety in his mind, it was cautiously concealed from the view of others.

"Well," said Mr. Conant, interrupting the silence, "even if Massasoit joins himself unto them, we are strong in numbers and doubly strong in the Lord of Hosts."

"The sachem of Mount Haup is true as the course of the sun," rejoined the Indian, somewhat indignant that his friendship should be doubted. "If an arrow comes among us, it comes from Corbitant's quiver. But though the rattlesnake's death be on its feather, the wise man must aim it, and the Good Spirit must wing it to the mark. When you pray to the Englishman'sGod, he sends your corn drink, and you say he make the waters in two tribes, for the white man to pass through. Is he not bigger than the Pequods and the Mohegans, the Narragansets and the Tarateens?"

Without waiting for an answer, he took up the cap which lay on the floor beside him, and left the house.

"It is a shame on us that an Indian must teach us who is 'our shield and our buckler," observed Mr. Conant. "To my mind there is more danger of Satan's killing us with the rat's–bane of toleration, than the Lord's taking us off with the Indian arrows. It behoveth the watchmen of Israel to be on their guard, for false prophets and false Christs are abroad in the land. 'One saith he is in the desert, and another saith he is in the secret chambers;' and much reason have the elect to laud the God of Israel, that his right hand

33

upholdeth them in slippery places."

"I am much in the dark whether you can clearly prove, from Scripture, that the elect are always upheld in slippery places," said Mr. Oldham. "What do you make of the falling off of Judas Iscariot?"

"What do I make of it, man? Why that he never was among the elect. Christ saith, "none of them have I lost but the son of perdition, that the Scriptures might be fulfilled."

"Why, Paul himself seems not to have been clear upon the subject," continued Mr. Oldham; "for he says, 'lest when I have preached unto others, I should myself prove a cast–away.' And know you not that God's chosen people staid so long in Egypt that they forgot the name of Jehovah? And what with the brick bondage of spiritual Egypt on the one hand, and the flesh–pots on the other, I think there is much danger that the elect may so lose the sound of his voice, that they will not know it, when it calls them from the four winds of heaven."

"I have found by experience," said Governor Endicott, "that the more doubts we let in at the floodgate, the faster gripe Satan hath upon our souls. St. Augustine hath it, 'Nullum malum pejus libertate errandi;' and I believe he is in the right."

"I don't know any thing about your outlandish tongue," replied Mr. Oldham; "and, I mean no disrespect to your Honor, but I think it savors of Babylon to be calling on the name of this saint and that saint. I marvel when christians have turned the pope out of doors, they don't send his rags out of the window. To my thinking, the devil will send him back again after his duds, forasmuch as they are suffered to remain in the church."

"Augustine was a holy man," rejoined Governor Endicott; "though in many things, the Lord suffered him to remain in darkness. He it was, who left a burning coal upon the altar, wherewithal Calvin and Luther lighted up the great fire of the Reformation; a fire which burneth yet, and which will burn, until Babylon be consumed, with her robes and her mitres, her cross and her staff, her bishops and her prelates, her masses and her mummeries. Yea, let the disciples of the hell–born Loyola strive against it as they will. But as for St. Augustine, my friend, you'll acknowledge the spirit of the matter to be good, though it is clothed in outlandish dress, when I tell you that it meaneth, 'there is no evil worse than the liberty of wandering."'

"There is much truth in that, no doubt," replied Mr. Graves; "but I maintain it is contrary to the declarations of Scripture, unless you can prove that it appertains to the unpardonable sin."

"St. Augustine probably wrote it without any especial reference to that passage," said the Governor.

"And I maintain that it's popish blasphemy to write any thing without an especial reference to the declarations of Scripture," replied his antagonist, who seemed to stand on the battle ground of controversy, calling out, like Goliah, 'Choose you a man for you, and let him come down to me that I may fight him.' "And as for you, Mr. Oldham, if you have such doubts as you've been speaking of, it is because you have sinned yourself into them; and I marvel if it be not by the leaven of idle words, and levity of speech."

"God gave us laughter as well as reason, to my apprehension," rejoined Mr. Oldham, "Solomon saith, 'there is a time for all things;' and the commentary that I put upon the text is, that there is a time to smoke a pipe and crack a joke, as well as to preach and pray."

"You know not what you say, nor whereof you affirm," answered Mr. Conant. "Recreation is no doubt good to oil the wheels as we travel along a rugged road; but a wise man will do as Jonathan, who only tasted a little honey on the end of his rod. As for that text of Solomon, it is a sort of flaming cherubim that turneth every way, and many a man hath it slain."

"I'm thinking at any rate," retorted Oldham, "that a scythe cuts the better, if a man stops to whet it atween whiles."

"That's true enough," replied he from the Isle of Wight, "but what would you say to see a man whetting his scythe the whole day instead of mowing? I tell you, Mr. Oldham, he that gives up, even for an hour; the blessed comforts of the gospel and the inward out—pouring of prayer, for the mere crackling thorns of worldly mirth, does but exchange his pearls for old iron."

"I think," interrupted Governor Endicott, "that there is much appertaining to error implied in the doctrine of inward outpouring. That egg was laid in the Netherlands, and if it be kept warm, I've a suspicion that the viper will hereafter spring out of its shell, and aim at the vitals of the church. It is a wandering meteor of human pride, and doth but serve to lead from the true light of revelation."

"Ah, it is a sad thing," observed Mr. Conant, "that before we have got the church of Christ well balanced, Satan, seeing the dominion of the beast going down in one quarter, straightway sendeth forth his ministers to and fro in the earth, and teacheth them to cry down Antichrist as much as the boldest of us, at the same time that they lead poor souls into more horrid blasphemies than the papist. These gross errors, broached in the dark, are sliding like the plague into the veins of the church; but in none of them the devil so plainly sheweth his horns, as in this doctrine of inward light."

"According to my notions," said Mr. Graves, scripture would be but a dead letter without inward light. I'm thinking a clock would be but a sorry thing, with its clever–figured face, if there was no wheel–work to set it agoing."

"Your comparison hath no savor of similitude," replied the Governor. "I grant there is a concealed life and spirit in the letter of the Bible; but God hath hidden it, and it is not for man to penetrate into the mysteries of godliness. The index of the clock sufficeth to do our daily work by, and is of no further use to him that knows the wheels which move it, than to him who never thought thereupon."

This probably would have paved the way for fresh controversy, had not the entrance of Hobomok interrupted the conversation. His appearance betrayedno marks of agitation, nor was any surprise excited when he stooped and spoke to the Governor, who immediately followed him out of the room. As soon as they were out of hearing, Hobomok told him his suspicions of Corbitant, and added that he was certain there were a number of Indians in ambush in the woods below. The chief magistrate determined at once that a company should be collected silently and speedily. Hobomok was deputed to give orders to several individuals to proceed to his house with as little appearance of alarm as possible; and the Indian set forth upon the expedition; first requesting the Governor not to lose sight of Mr. Conant's house. When Governor Endicott returned to the company he had left, he stated the fears of their Indian friend as gently as possible; but cautiously as they were told, it proved too much for the weak nerves of Mrs. Conant. Since her residence in the wilderness, alarms of this kind had been frequent, and she had borne them with fortitude; but now the body weighed down the firmness of the soul; and her husband was obliged to leave his fainting wife to the care of her daughter, with an assurance that their safety should be cared for. They were indeed well protected; for Hobomok, the moment his errands were hastily delivered, had returned to guard them with the quick eye of love, and the ready arm of hatred.

The company so suddenly collected, pursued a circuitous rout, and came at once upon the unguarded enemy. The band which they discovered consisted of twenty Indians, most of whom were petty sachems of Massasoit, who had been wrought upon by the eloquence of Corbitant, for the purpose of setting fire to Mr. Conant's house, and murdering the inhabitants, if possible.

From his own account, it seemed that Mr. Conant's quotation with regard to the arrows being broken at Salem, had been construed by Corbitant into a defiance of the neighbouring tribes; and that he had taken this step to revenge the insult; however, it is probable that the blow was aimed, through them, at the heart of Hobomok. Ambush and stratagem are the pride of Indian warfare, and now that their designs were so completely traversed, they attempted no resistance. The captives were placed in an enclosed piece of public land, and a guard of thirty men set over them. Mr. Conant returned to his family, and Mary, inured to such occurrences, slept peacefully within their humble dwelling, unconscious that Hobomok watched it the livelong night, with eyes that knew no slumber. Every man saw that his gun was loaded and his pistols within reach; and at midnight nothing was seen in motion but the sentinels, as they passed backward and forward, their arms gleaming in the moon.

CHAP. VI.

```
If heaven a draught of heavenly pleasure spare,
One cordial in this melancholy vale,
'Tis when a youthful, loving, modest pair,
In other's arms breathe out the tender tale,
Beneath the milk-white thorn that scents the evening gale.
    — Burns.
```

The dawn presented a scene unusual to the inhabitants of Salem. The prisoners, some standing erect, some seated on the ground, and others leaning upon their bows, wore one uniform expression of defiance and rage. The Englishmen who stood around them, resting on their loaded guns, had that look of peculiarghastliness which the light of

37

morning gives to men who have passed a sleepless and anxious night. However, the sun had hardly placed his golden circlet on the summit of the highest eastern hills, before the deep rolling of the drum was heard along the street, and fresh recruits passed on, to take the place of their companions. In the mean time a council was called at the chief magistrate's, to determine what should be done with the prisoners.

"My countrymen," said Governor Endicott, "you all know for what purpose you are now called hither. Well it is for us that our brethren from the Isle of Wight have arrived among us; inasmuch as the wickedness of Morton hath made these savages very daring of late. But, as I was about to say, while we were sitting in the house of Mr. Conant, talking of God, and the things appertaining to salvation, Hobomok came among us and gave warning of a party of Indians in the hollow; forasmuch as he, whom we all know the Lord hath gifted with great quickness of ear, heard a low whoop therefrom. You know how the thing hath proved, and how wonderfully we have been saved from the malice and stratagems of our enemies; and now I would fain ask your judgment concerning what is best to be done in this matter."

After some discussion it was determined that Mr. Conant should take with him a strong guard, and convey the captives to their head sachem, Massasoit. Upon which, their godly minister, Mr. Higginson, arose and desired them to join with him in a petition to the throne of grace. Every hat was reverently laid aside, and a short, impressive prayer was made with the involuntary eloquence of recent gratitude. A strong guard was equipped, and as they passed in review before the Governor, the ensign stepped out anddelivered the colors of the red cross, which had been unfurled the night before.

"It is marvellous in my eyes that the Lord fighteth on our side, while we march under such a badge of Antichrist," said Governor Endicott. "It as much beseemeth a christian to carry the half–moon of Mahomet, as such an emblem of popish victory. However, the pleasure of the king be obeyed."

Hobomok, who had been waiting for "the council fire to be extinguished," fell into the rear of the company, and re–conducted Mr. Collier to Plymouth.

During several hours the settlement continued in that state of excitement which might naturally be supposed to follow an alarm so unexpected. All the people that were near, called at Mr. Conant's, one after another, to hear the extent of the danger to which they had been exposed, till Mary and her mother were weary of repeating the story.

"I have come hither to find out the root of the matter," Madam Conant, said a neighbouring widow. "I heard last night that there was three hundred Indians found in Endicott's Hollow; and there I sat trembling afraid to venture out, till Jacob came home and told me something about the business."

"And I," observed another, "heard that Corbitant shot Governor Endicott in the mouth. Oh, it was a woful night to us women folks who have just come among you. We never hear of such like proceedings in our island."

"The matter hath no doubt been much magnified," replied Mrs. Conant. "We have reason to be thankful the Indians were few and easily surprised. But here is neighbour Oldham, who was one of the company. He can tell you every thing connected therewith."

"There was but one arrow fired," said Mr. Oldham; "and, as the Lord would have it, that stuck fast in a bit of cheese rind in my jacket pocket. Which, I think, proveth good the old saying, that 'a little armour serveth a man if he knoweth where to put it.' But, after all our affrightment, this hath proved a small matter. The Lord hath merely given us a jog on the elbow at this time; that we may remember the dangers wherewithal we are surrounded, and wake up our sluggish souls, that have become somewhat perfunctory in his service."

"That's what my good man said, when he was dying," rejoined the widow. "Poor soul, the Indian shot him through and through, when he was digging for clams in the sands down there at Plymouth; and when I pulled out the arrow and bound up his wounds, he told me, it was all a chastisement of the Lord, in that we had fallen into rebellious ways."

"And I remember as well as if it was but yesterday," said another, "how my poor Joseph looked in them dreadful times. A bright and handsome boy he was once, but he overworked himself; and then he grew poor, and pale as a ghost, and what was worst of all, I hadn't food wherewithal to keep life in his body."

"Ah there is nobody knows the troubles and distresses of a new settlement, but those who have tasted thereof," observed Mrs. Conant; and she paused and sighed deeply, as the painful remembrance of her own lost sons passed before her. "But one must not talk of their own griefs at such a time," continued she. "There is great commotion throughout the

39

world; and it is plain to perceive that Jehovah is shaking the heavens above our head, and the earth beneath our feet."

"Ay, ay," answered Oldham, "these are fearsome times in church and state, when the domineering bishop of London, whom no godly man ever yet knew without giving laud to the devil by reason of the acquaintance. I say it is fearful times when such like men have power to drive God's heritage into the wilderness, where they must toil hard for a scanty bread, and that too with daily jeopardy of life and limb."

"And they tell me likewise," rejoined Mrs. Conant "that Sir Ferdinando Gorges is likely to make difficulty about the Massachusetts patent; and that the Lord, for further trial of our faith, hath suffered more enemies to be stirred up against us in England, who are ready, like Amalek of old, to smite Israel while they are weak and unable for defence."

"Oh yes," replied Mr. Oldham; "and the Earl of Warwick, and divers other great folks who hold possessions here, 'sit under their vine and their fig–tree, with none to molest or make them afraid,' and little know they concerning our troubles, and never a hand of theirs would ward off a blow, unless where the matter of filthy lucre was concerned."

"Nevertheless," said Mrs. Conant, "the work will prosper. Though there appeareth now but a little cloud, about the bigness of a man's hand; yet the Lord Christ is in it, and out of it shall shine the perfection of beauty."

"I could listen to your edifying discourse all the day long, but there is no time for folding of hands now–a–days," interrupted the widow, as she threw her cloak over her shoulders. "My red cardinal is over warm for the season to be sure, but then I think it is but decent to have something over a body's head."

"I marvel that you should think it decent to call a christian garment by a name that appertains to the scarlet woman of Babylon," said Mr. Oldham.

"It's no name of my making, Goodman; nor did I know that evil was signified thereby," answered the widow. "But I must be stirring homewards. The Lord bless you all."

The other visitors gradually followed her example, and quietness and order were soon restored to the household.

Hobomok

"Mother," said Mary, after their guests had all departed, "you know father has gone to Plymouth for two or three days?"

"To be sure I do, my child," replied Mrs. Conant, smiling. "And what then?" Mary hesitated a few moments ere she added, "I have seen Charles Brown this morning; and he is coming here this evening, that is, if you have no objection thereto."

"You well know my heart, my dear Mary," replied her mother, "but I ought not to do wrong because your father is absent."

"You don't think it is wrong—in your conscience you can't think it's wrong," said Mary, as she kissed her forehead, and looked up archly in her face. "So do say he may come."

"You have sacrificed much for me, my child," answered the indulgent parent. And, pausing a moment, she continued, "Perhaps I do wrong thus to violate the injunctions of my husband, but I know you are prudent, and you may e'en follow your own dictates concerning this matter."

The young man to whom we have so often referred, was a graduate at Oxford, and of no ordinary note in his native kingdom. He had known Mary before she left the mansion of her noble grandfather; and the remembrance of the little fairy just blushing into womanhood had proved powerful enough to draw the ambitious young lawyer from the fair hopes of distinction in England, to the wild and romantic schemeof establishing the Episcopal mitre in the forests of America. The state in which he found things on his arrival, induced him to abandon his favorite project; and prudence for awhile enabled him to conceal his high church principles. But the crown and the mitre were interwoven with every association of his heart, and in that hot–bed of argument he found the attempt at neutrality was in vain. Notwithstanding the first settlers at Naumkeak had taken the liberty of nonconforming to the rules of their mother church, and to the established regulations of the Plymouth elders, Mr. Brown soon found that they complained loudly of the spirit of the times. Mr. Conant in particular, stated that New England was likely to become "a cage for every unclean bird. A free stable–room and litter for all kinds of consciences." Such expressions extorted from Brown an involuntary reproach upon those false guides who had first taught men to wander from the true church. This was, of course, the watch–word of animosity; and from that time the young man was considered as Ishmael in the house of Abraham. However, long after the old man discovered the abomination of his sentiments, he continued a daily visitor at Mr. Conant's, who 'felt it his duty to controvert the matter with him, inasmuch as the Lord might please to make him the instrument of his redemption." But it could not long remain concealed that metal more attractive than the iron glove of controversy, had drawn him to their fire–side; and, with more anger than Mrs. Conant had ever before seen him manifest, he forbade him the house forever.

With all Mary's habitual sweetness of disposition, this course of conduct did serve to diminish her filial respect and affection. She had no sympathy with her father's religious scruples, for her heart very naturally bowed down before the same altar with the man she loved. None could form an idea of the depth and fervor of her affection, who had not, like her, left a bright and sunny path, to wander in the train of misery, gloom, and famine. During her stay at her grandfather's, she had become familiar with much that was beautiful in painting, and lovely in sculpture, as well as all that was elegant in the poetry of that early period; and their rich outline was deeply impressed upon her young heart. For her mother's sake, she endured the mean and laborious offices which she was obliged to perform, but she lived only in the remembrance of that fairy spot in her existence. Alone as she was, without one spirit that came in contact with her own, she breathed only in the regions of fancy; and many an ideal object had she invested with its rainbow robe. When at length she found a being who understood her feelings, and who loved, as she had imagined love, her whole soul was rivetted. The harshness of her father tended to increase this, by rendering the stream of affection more undivided in its source. In such a state of things, their interviews must of course be transient and unfrequent; but when they did occur, the cup of joy, so seldom tasted, sparkled to the brim. Let the philosopher say what he will about these humbler blossoms of the heart, earth has nothing like them, for loveliness and fragrance. And he, who through the dim lapse of years, remembers the time when two full, gushing tides of young affection, were mingled in one common stream, will hardly be willing to acknowledge that the world is altogether "vanity and vexation of spirit."

The remembrance of her own thwarted inclinations wrought powerfully on the mind of Mary's gentle and affectionate mother, and she at length gave their meeting her unqualified consent. The bowl of chocolate was prepared that night with even more careful fondness than usual; and as Mrs. Conant at an early hour laid her head upon the pillow, she was just preparing to say, "I fear I do wrong, my child," but Mary kissed away the sentence.

Hobomok

The absence of so many of the inhabitants, and the fear of some fresh alarm, made it expedient that the outskirts of the settlement should be guarded, and Mary well knew that Brown was on that duty. In expectation of his arrival, she stationed herself at the door, and looked out upon the still brightness around. The lonely spot was fair and tranquil, and earth, sea, and sky, beneath the unvaried radiance of the moon, "seemed just waking from some heavenly dream." The evening star was sailing along its peaceful course, and seemed, amid the stainless sanctity of the heavens, like a bright diadem on the brow of some celestial spirit. "Fair planet," thought Mary, "how various are the scenes thou passest over in thy shining course. The solitary nun, in the recesses of her cloister, looks on thee as I do now; mayhap too, the courtly circle of king Charles are watching the motion of thy silver chariot. The standard of war is fluttering in thy beams, and the busy merchantman breaks thy radiance on the ocean. Thou hast kissed the cross–crowned turrets of the Catholic, and the proud spires of the Episcopalian. Thou hast smiled on distant mosques and temples, and now thou art shedding the same light on the sacrifice heap of the Indian, and the rude dwellings of the Calvinist. And can it be, as my father says, that of all the multitude of people who view thy cheering rays, so small a remnant only are pleasing in the sight of God? Oh, no. It cannot be thus. Would that my vision, like thine, could extend through the universe, that I might look down unmovedon the birth and decay of human passions, hopes, and prejudices."

These thoughts were interrupted by the appearance of Brown, as he came whistling along the footpath, the light of evening resting full upon his handsome features.

"The moon has seemed to rise slowly and wearily since I have been looking out for you," said the maiden, as her lover gaily imprinted a kiss upon her hand.

"I could wish she would stop her shining course awhile," replied he; "for, setting aside the expectation of meeting you, it is one of the brightest nights I ever looked upon."

"I have been watching it," answered Mary, "till it hath almost made me sad. At this moment she is shining on the lordly palaces and blooming gardens of good old England, is she not?"

"Ah yes; and such thoughts make even my heart sicken within me. But it is not so when I think of you. Love 'maketh the desert to blossom as the rose.' Besides, my dear Mary, I trust we shall both live in England again."

Hobomok

"Never while my mother lives, Charles. I would not leave her even for you. But she will soon go from us to be no more. I picked a little shivering violet the other day, and it seemed the sweeter for the cold dew that was on it. And I thought it was so like to my mother; for the sicker she is, the more she seemeth like an angel."

I know not why it is, but, in minds of a certain tone, the richest melody of love is always mingled with notes of sadness; and, in the full communion of unreserved tenderness, the maiden leaned her head upon the shoulder of the young man, and wept in silence.

"My dear Mary," said Brown, "it is not well to be melancholy. We both ought to recollect that thereis One above who will defend us, though every earthly friend be taken. As for your father, he may be conscientious in this matter; but I more than half suspect that he cares more about having his own way, than he does for all the prayers and churches in christendom. If so, I know your kind mother will use all her influence to overcome his obstinacy."

"I know it too," replied Mary; "but her counsels have little weight with him when he has determined upon a course. However, he loves her; and I believe she loves him as well as she ever could in her earliest days."

"Do you think you could endure so much for me, Mary?" asked her lover, while his bright dark eye rested with more than usual admiration on the passive beauty of her countenance.

"A cold heart may make promises and protestations," she replied; "and when we dream of love we are always too apt to think of the paradise, rather than the thorny hedge which the sin of Adam has placed around it; but let the storm come upon you, Charles, and see if my head shrink from the tempest."

"I know by experience how hard it is to escape from the entanglements of the heart," answered Brown. "My life was full of enjoyment before I met you in Lincolnshire; and now, when I try to think of any source of happiness in which you have no share, I am forced to acknowledge that you are, in some way or other, connected therewith. You remember that those who entered Spencer's shady grove,

Whose loftie trees yelad with sommer's pride,

44

Did spred so broad, that heaven's light did hide,

Not perceable with power of any starr;

When weening to returne whence they did straye,

They cannot finde that path which once was showne,

But wander to and fro in waies unknowne.

"And isn't it so with the path of love, my Mary?"

A smiling glance from the bright eye of the maiden gave an answer of silent eloquence. The interview was prolonged to a late hour; and the conversation of the lovers became gradually more and more marked by that tenderness of expression, which, "like the rich wines of the south, is so delicious in its native soil; so tasteless in the transportation."

CHAP. VII.

"The church was umpire then."

Among all the varieties of human character, from the refined enthusiast in classic literature, down to the ignoramus who signs a cross in behoof of his name, there are very few who have strength enough to resist the flattering suffrage of exclusive preference. Gratified vanity proves a powerful pleader in most hearts upon such occasions; and if love itself be not induced, the resemblance passes for awhile as current coin. I say for awhile, for most of the unhappy marriages which have come under my own observation, have originated in this mistake. However, I shall not stop to moralize upon the subject. Suffice it to say, that Collier, under the dominion of such feelings, returned to Plymouth with a lightsome and happy heart; nothing disturbed, save by his anticipated eclaircissement with Hopkins. Much as he dreaded the interview, he found his friend even more unwilling to relinquish his claims, than he had expected.

The low, flat–roofed fort of Plymouth, and the adjacent wigwam of Hobomok, were just rising on the sight, when the anxious young man came out to meet them.

Hobomok

"What's the news, John?" inquired he.

"That twenty Indians have been surprised in a plan of setting fire to the house of that wise and godly man, Mr. Roger Conant," rejoined the traveller. "They are this day sent, under guard, to the sachem of Mount Haup; and with them we came some ways in company."

"Ah, indeed," replied Hopkins. "I thought the Indians were quiet enough of late; but it is plain there will be no peace in the land while Corbitant is therein. That sachem is a hot–headed fellow, and implacable withal. Albeit," continued he, as they entered the house, "I will hear your Indian stories at a more convenient season. What did Sally say, when she found she had been thought of these three years, and she all the while knew nothing about the matter?"

"Why, to speak the truth, James, I have no very pleasant duty to perform in this business; for the damsel hath expressly declared, she doth not look upon you with as favorable eyes as upon some others."

"That's what they always say," answered the confident lover. "Peradventure she thinks that dear bought goods are most valued. I tell you, man, she hath expressed her liking for me a hundred times, and would now, if you had been bold in the business."

"Hath she?" inquired his messenger. "Bethink you, Hopkins; hath she ever told you she loved you before others?"

"A hundred times," replied he. "That is, I mean,— you know I don't mean,—I would'nt say it if I did—that she hath done so unbecoming a thing as to tell me she would marry me, before she knew whether I would or no; but, nevertheless, I repeat she hath said it a hundred times over, by her looks and actions. And I should like to know, forsooth, whom she may prefer to me, in this wilderness? Haven't I loved her these three years? And didn't I do all I could for 'em when the elders saw fit to dismiss her father? And haven't I put up the best house in Plymouth, wherewithal to please her?"

"I know all that," rejoined his friend; "and assuredly I thought your suit would be favorably received. I marvel that it was not; but I had as good tell it at once, as not.—The maiden hath declared she loveth another man better."

46

Hobomok

"And I should like to know who it might be?" said the indignant lover.

The young man judged by his countenance, that he was "nursing his wrath to keep it warm," and he felt more and more the awkwardness of his ungracious mission. He blushed, stammered, hesitated, and finally answered, "The maiden told me in express words, that if you and I had changed places, the messenger would have returned with 'yea' in his mouth."

Mr. Hopkins turned his face toward the window, and bit his thumb some time, without speaking a word.

"I suppose you will take it unkind," observed Collier, interrupting the silence. "But what could be done in such a case?"

"Talk to me no more about it," replied the disappointed suitor. "I am not the man to break my heart about a foolish damsel. If she pleases to shape her course in this way, I can assure her there is no love lost between us. But after all, Collier, this is a confounded unfriendly job, on your part; and I shall state as much to the church."

"I beg of you not to make the the affair public," said his friend; "if you will hear to reason, you will see I could not have done otherwise than I have."

"I don't want to hear any reasons about it," retorted his offended companion. "I tell you once more, I don't care a pin concerning the matter; but when I see wolves walking about in sheep's clothing, I'll e'en strip off their fleece." And without waiting for an answer, he took up his hat and walked out of the house. He had said and thought that he cared nothing about his disappointment; but when he was alone, and all restraint of manly pride was removed, he found that the thread, so unexpectedly broken, was interwoven with the whole web of his existence; and spite of himself, a few reluctant tears rolled down his weather–beaten face. However, resentment was uppermost; and the following day his rival was summoned to appear before the church, to answer certain charges brought against him by James Hopkins. Collier would gladly have avoided a public conference on such a subject, but under existing circumstances, there was but one alternative. He must either suffer under a suspicion of his good faith, or he must candidly state events as they happened. In these degenerate times, when even plighted love is broken with such frequent impunity, it would excite a smile to have seen the elderly men assembled at Mr.

Brewster's, and with serious aspects discussing so important an affair. But in those days, the church kept careful watch upon the out−goings and in−comings of her children, and suffered not the pollution of a butterfly's feather to rest upon her garments.

After the disputants were seated, the worthy clergyman began;

"It is with much grief we notice the falling out of two godly young men, sons of right worthy gentlemenamong us. Especially as one is accused of having dealt treacherously with the other, and spoken deceitful words unto him."

Then Mr. Collier answered; "I feel it is an unpleasant duty to vindicate myself from this aspersion, inasmuch as Mr. Hopkins is my valued friend, and hath been somewhat too hasty in this matter, refusing to hear explanations which I have sought to give unto him. I likewise think that the things appertaining to love are of too light a nature to be brought before the church, that they should discuss thereupon. But that you may know that in nothing have I dealt treacherously with my friend, you shall hear the conclusion of the whole matter. Hearing that the vessels were soon to leave Naumkeak, and having business wherewithal they were connected, I had a mind to take Hobomok for my guide, and journey thither. Whereupon Mr. Hopkins gave me a letter for Mr. Oldham's daughter (whom you all know is a comely damsel, and, withal of a cheerful behaviour); which letter I delivered to the same, and asked an answer thereto. Then she said to me, that had I sent by Mr. Hopkins, instead of he by me, she should verily have said, 'I will go.' I spoke much to her concerning my friend's merits, but finding her mind was determined in this matter, I e'en told her I would have come out to meet her, as Isaac of old, when he brought the daughter of Bethuel into his tent. The maiden, you know, is well to look upon, and altogether such an one as no man need be averse to, as an help−meet. Now whether or not guile be found in me, I leave to your judgments; and if you so decide, I'm willing to be lopped off, as an unworthy member, from the church of Christ gathered in this place."

"Hear him," interrupted Hopkins. "He saith not a word about relinquishing the damsel. It seems hehad even rather be cast out as 'an heathen and a publican.' His love must have grown up wonderous sudden; for he denieth that he bewitched her with love potions, and implieth that when he went to Naumkeak he had no thoughts save of procuring her for my wife."

"I not only imply it," answered Collier, "but I expressly declare that I then had no thought respecting her wherewithal you were not connected. And now I do truly say, that I had rather be sent out from among my brethren, although it would be very grievous unto me, than to dismiss the maiden, whom of a surely, I do regard with much complacency since she hath so declared her sentiments."

"Of a truth, I see nothing wherein you have erred, according to your own account," observed elder Brewster; "but there is a gentleman soon going to Naumkeak, to convey a letter from our honorable chief magistrate to the reverend Mr. Higginson, respecting the baptism of his son, and, for the further satisfaction of Mr. Hopkins, it may be well that he return with a written statement of facts. Till which time, we do defer our decision."

Poor Sally was in great consternation when the Plymouth messenger arrived, and informed her of the serious aspect which the business had assumed.

"Oh, Mary," said she, "what shall I do? You know that Mr. Hopkins who bawled himself into love with me, and had'nt courage to sing the last note after all? Well, he has made a great fuss between Mr. Collier and the church, and they have sent to me to write all that I said concerning him."

"I always wondered how you could have spoken to Mr. Collier after such a fashion," replied Mary. "I see nothing you can do but to write the whole truth."

"Will you write it for me?"

"Oh, yes, if you'll provide words to the purpose."

So the pen and ink was brought forward, and Mary wrote a letter which she indited as follows:

"Reverende Sirs,

"Wheras Mr. Collier hathe beene supposed to blame concerning some businesse he hath of late endeavoured to transacte for Mr. Hopkins, this cometh to certifie that he did faithfully performe his dutie, and moreover that his great modestie did prevente his understanding many hints, until I spoke even as he hath represented. Wherefore, if there be oughte unseemly in this, it lieth on my shoulders.

"With all dutie and respecte, ""Sally X Oldham. "Her marke."

N. B. "Sence my Dawter hathe shewed mee this Yepistall I dwoe furthere righte with my owne Hande a feu wordes of Add vice untwoe you att Plimouth, respecting Churche Govermente. Twoe my thinking you runn ewer Horses over harde, draweinge the Ranes soe tite, thatt maybee thale rair upp and caste thare rideers intwoe the mudd. U may rubb folkse Nose on the Grinnstone thinking to ware them twoe the Gristell, and in the eende you maye make them twoe Sharppe for ewer owne cumfurt. Dwoe nott constrew this intwoe Dishrespecte from hymm whoe hathe mutch Occashun to remember thatt you awl gave hymm a helping Hande in the Race he runn among you. U sea by this thatt I am noe Skribe and you new heretoefore thatt I was noe Farisee.

"john Oldham."

Upon the receipt of this document, the elders thought fit to take no notice of Mr. Oldham's advice, though all thought it contained too much of his accustomed impudence. Sally's testimony was so simple and decisive, that Mr. Brewster at once gave a concluding answer.

"Although we deem it unseemly for young women to pursue such like courses (indeed were she within our jurisdiction, we should give her public reproof therefor), and though we do fear that the daughter hath much of the corrupt leaven of the father, yet we do not see that we have a right to constrain the consciences of men in these particulars, especially as the apostle saith 'the believing husband may sanctify the unbelieving wife.' Therefore, we do leave Mr. Collier to pursue whatsoever course he deemeth expedient, trusting that, whatever he doth, he will do it in the name of the Lord. Moreover, we do think it proper that Mr. Hopkins make an apology to him, inasmuch as he hath not been slow to anger, nor charitable concerning his brother in the church."

The penance was performed with as good a grace as could be expected, and the young men returned to their respective employments.

CHAP. VIII.

Take her, she's thy wife.
  — Shakspeare

It may easily be imagined how things continued at Salem for several succeeding weeks. Mr. Collier was as frequent a visitor as distance and difficulty of travellingwould permit; Hobomok divided his time almost equally between his mother's wigwam, and the dwelling of Mr. Conant; and Mary obtained a "paradisaical interview" with Brown, as often as possible; Mrs. Conant, sinking in a slow, but certain decline, seemed

"Like a spirit who longs for a purer day,

And is ready to wing her flight away;"

her husband, prudent, moderate, and persevering in public affairs,—at home, sometimes passionate, and always unyielding; and Mr. Oldham, the same as ever, an odd mixture of devotion and drollery.

The manuscript mentions numerous controversies between Mr. Higginson, Mr. Conant, Mr. Oldham, and Mr. Graves; but their character is so similar to those I have already quoted, that I forbear to repeat them. One maintained justification by faith, and another by works; and the light–within–enthusiast, from the Isle of Wight, continued to defend his doctrine of the inward outpouring of prayer, and eventually became one of the most celebrated among the Familists.

Sally listened to all their arguments with heedless gaiety; Mary heard their wild war of words, with increased weariness; and as her noble mother approached the confines of another world, and received its calm, heavenly influence, she looked with compassion on the wild and ever–varying light of human doctrines.

But while things remained unaltered in these two families, the spirit of improvement was rapidly extending in the village, and the young English lawyer had commenced his efforts for the establishment of the Episcopal church. He met with a hearty co–operation from his brother Samuel, who had been a merchant of high respectability in his native land, and from Mr. Blackstone, the solitary hermit at Tri–Mountain, who originally came to

51

America with the same design. These movements, of course, called forth all the energy of the non—conformists, and consequently the number of Brown's adherents increased; for the love of excitement is a fundamental principle in the human mind, and men will seek it wherever it is to be found;—whether in the contests of gladiators, the clashing of arms, the painful power of tragic representation, or the tumultuous zeal of jarring sectaries.

Things were in this state, when it was announced in three successive meetings,

"Be it known unto all, that John Collier of Plymouth, and Sally Oldham of Salem, are about to enter into the holy state of wedlock. If any man hath objection, let him proclaim it publicly."

No man, excepting Mr. Thomas Graves, had any objection, and on the 5th of August a small company collected at Mr. Oldham's, to witness the bridal. Mrs. Conant claimed the privilege of giving the wedding gown, a beautiful chintz, adorned with flowers even larger than life, which had been a favorite morning dress with the Lady Mary before her marriage. Governor Endicott, likewise, "though he approved not of the drinking of wine, and had abolished it at his own table, yet he could not forbear sending a little on this occasion, inasmuch as it was the first wedding they had had among them." The manuscript mentions the chief magistrate as "bolde and undaunted, yet sociable, and of a cheerful spirite, loving or austere, as occasion served." On the day of the wedding he unbent his stateliness more than usual, and held much courteous discourse with Mr. Conant's and Mr. Oldham's families, while the young couple sat beside each other, silently and timidly waiting for the arrival of Mr. Higginson. Mary sat on the lefthand of the bride, and their countenances, both interesting, presented a striking contrast of beauty. Sally's clear, rosy complexion was becomingly heightened by the excitement of her wedding day; her bright, roguish blue eyes sparkled; and her round, Hebe form appeared to the utmost advantage in her handsome dress. In short she seemed the living, laughing representation of health. But Mary's slender figure, her large, dark eyes, with their deep, melancholy fringe, and the graceful carriage of her neck and shoulders, brought before the mind a Parian statue, or one of those fair visions which fancy gives to slumber. The old men gazed on them in their loveliness, and turned away with that deep and painful sigh, which the gladness of childhood, and the transient beauty of youth, are so apt to awaken in the bosom of the aged. "Alas, that things so fair should be so fleeting," has been repeated thousands of times; and yet how keenly it still enters into the soul, when early fascinations have faded away, and imagination has scattered her garland to the winds. Who has looked on young, sunny smiles, and listened to loud, merry tones, without a feeling almost amounting to anguish, when he has thought of the temptations which would infest their path, and the disappointments which would inevitably crush their budding hopes? Perhaps these ideas, under various modifications, might be the reason of the general silence, for every one seemed fearful of hearing his own voice. Even Sally's giddy temper seemed to be wholly subdued by the solemnity of the vow she was about to take. She sat reserved and diffident, and a crowd of thoughts pressed upon her mind, till she hardly knew whether they were pleasant or painful. At length, however, she ventured to raise her hand to her mouth, and whisper to Mary, "I asked Brown to come to–day; and then I told himnot to come; because it would make trouble for you." The ice once broken, whispers were soon heard around the room, and presently Mr. Conant rose and took two or three turns through the apartment, and looked out of the window, as he said, "We shall have a favorable day for our ordination to–morrow, God willing. But they tell me we are to be pestered with the presence of the papistical Mr. Blackstone."

"Well, if he cometh hither, I'll give him the plague, if I can catch it for him," said Mr. Oldham. "They tell me he giveth much countenance to Brown's untoward company."

"It was said in Lincolnshire," observed Mary, who was anxious to change the conversation, "that love was the occasion of his coming hither; and that if a young lady in Huntingdonshire had smiled upon him, he had not been thus wedded to his canonical robe."

"I never heard of a man's being crazy, or in any wise straying from the common path," replied Mr. Oldham, "but that some pretty piece of Eve's flesh, with a head as empty as a New England purse (and it cannot well be emptier), hath straightway supposed herself the cause thereof. Their vanity is as long as the polar nights, and as broad as a Puritan's shoulders need to be. Here is Sally now, who for a wonder is as demure as you please, has thought her carcass such a valuable cargo that every body she sees must needs want the freight. And her head, no doubt is somewhat higher with her Egyptian garments."

"Say nothing about the dress, my friend," interrupted the Governor. "A goodly book should have a comely covering; and as for these women, it is as well to let them alone. It is meet they should stand by themselves, like Quæ Genus in the Grammar; being deficients or redundants, not to be brought under any rule whatsoever."

"Yes, there is many a queer genius among 'em," answered Mr. Oldham; "and deficient enough in all conscience. But as to the subject that we were speaking of, I am wearied with these Episcopalians, who have come hither to make God's temple a dancing school for the devil."

"No doubt they will work their own destruction, and be caught in their own snare," said the Governor.

"Oh yes;" replied Oldham, "the devil will get out of breath with them in good time. I trow, he is broken-winded already with their prelatical galloping. I wish somebody would give them such a helping hand as I had during my race at Plymouth. I believe I have told you, Governor Endicott, concerning the comforting passages of scripture which the butt end of their muskets brought to my mind. It isn't every man who finds such a boost to his heavy heels. I mean no offence to you, Mr. Collier, but I am thinking if they buckle the girth much tighter, the horse will grow kickish. Come, laugh and be jolly, man— It is your wedding day—and such a day does not often come in a body's pilgrimage. But here cometh Mr. Higginson at last."

The reverend clergyman apologized for his delay, and entered into a conversation concerning the necessary preparations for the anticipated ordination. Mr. Oldham was evidently disposed for a merry-making; but a glance from his matronly dame, and the solemn tones of Mr. Higginson's voice, served to counteract the propensity.

He threw one knee over the other, drew in his lips, and passed his hand over his face, to cover it with the coat of sobriety. But the attempt was in vain, for in his most serious moods his mouth looked as if it contained an imprisoned laugh, which was struggling hard to make its escape from his small, black, piercing eyes.

The bride and bridegroom were soon requested to "stand before the holy man," and pronounce the vow which was to fix the coloring of their future lives. Sally went through the ceremony with modest propriety, and when they were pronounced "man and wife," many a one said, "They're a comely couple; and no doubt the Lord will bless them." Mr. Higginson sat in front of the young couple, and gave them much fatherly advice; which by the way is never less attended to, than at such a period. The bride sat picking the corner of her handkerchief, and seemed to listen with becoming reverence, though in fact she thought not a word about the discourse excepting to wish in mercy that it was concluded. At length, however, the friendly admonitions of the good man were exhausted, and wine, which had never before been drunk in that cottage, was handed to the guests. The older part of the company soon retired, and the young visitors gave themselves up to something like merriment.

CHAP. IX.

```
I seek divine simplicity in him,
Who handles things divine.
    — Cowper
```

Such a settlement as Salem during the summer of 1629, would seem insignificant enough to modern eyes; but compared with what it had been, it seemed rich and populous. Instead of the six miserable hovels,which it presented in June, there were now to be seen a number of comfortable dwellings, and a respectable edifice which served for various public uses. To Mr. Conant and his three solitary associates, were now added a large number of robust men, with their sober matrons and blooming daughters. And the place which a few months before had only echoed the occasional sound of the axe, or the shrill whoop of the hunter, was now busy with the hum of industry, and the clear, loud laughter of youth. With a decorum which characterized all the New England villages, they early began to arrange matters for the regular organization of a church. Two silenced non–conformists, Mr. Francis Higginson and Mr. Skelton, had arrived in the same vessel with my ancestor. Since that period they had been engaged in a controversial discussion with the Plymouth elders respecting church discipline, and at length, their jarring opinions being carefully balanced, on the 6th of August one was ordained teacher, and the other pastor of the church in Salem. Numerous were the preparations, both important and minute, for the solemnities of that day. Governor Bradford and his assistants, together with the clergy, were invited from Plymouth. Birds were brought down from their flight, and beasts slain for the occasion. The loaded fire–places sent forth a savory incense; and despite of the admonitions of their parents, there was as much "outward adorning, plaiting of the hair," as the slender wardrobe of the maidens would permit. The day was rich in cloudless, autumnal beauty. It seemed as if radiant spirits were gazing from the battlements of heaven upon a bright and happy world. It is astonishing with what facility we accommodate all the scenes of nature to our own state of feeling; so that beauty seems almost like an ideal outline, changing beneath the capricioushand of association,—meeting the eye, but to take its coloring from the heart. The feelings of the young bride involuntarily danced in sympathetic buoyancy with the season, though she saw nothing in it save promised abundance. To Mary, its full maturity seemed but the shadow of coming decay; and her dark eye rested upon Brown, as he walked before her in manly elegance, with a chastened tenderness that partook of sadness. Many a stolen glance was exchanged between the young men and maidens on their way to church, and with many a low courtesy and reverential bow, were the gentlemen in black saluted as they passed along. The assembly were at length collected, and with serious, staid deportment, awaited the commencement of the services. The Plymouth elders, detained by contrary winds, had not yet arrived, and there was a long pause of expectation, during which nothing was heard except the occasional movements of the sentinel, as he stood at the open door of the building. It was, indeed, a strange sight to see men in the house of God with pistols in their sword belts; but alarms from the Indians were then so much to be dreaded, that the protection of the Bible needed the aid of dagger and firelock. However, the expected brethren arrived not, and wearied with the delay, Mr. Higginson arose and made a solemn and impressive prayer. A psalm was then read by Mr. Skelton; and though in the music which followed there was no deep–toned organ to dive down into the recesses of the soul, and carry from thence man's warmest aspirations after heaven, yet there were some fine tones, which struck upon the ear in their bold harmony. And now every one was preparing to give earnest and devout attention to the reverend speaker, who was about to name his text; for in those days a sermon was an exhilarating draught, though convertedby the impious chemistry of modern times into a soporific drug. Notwithstanding it was loaded with some dozens of doctrines, and more uses than twenty sermons of these days will ever arrive at, and an improvement at the close, and a finally at the end of that, yet the manuscript asserts, that "the eies of men slumbered nott, neither were they wearie with hearing." Indeed the appearance of the learned and pious minister predisposed the mind to attention. His manner was dignified and simple; and as he rose to speak, he seemed bowed down with a humble and conscientious sense of his own unworthiness. Encumbered as I have mentioned, it cannot be supposed that the whole sermon would be interesting even to the antiquarian; but as a specimen of the eloquence of those times, I cannot forbear a few extracts.

"My text," said he, "is in the 105th Psalm, 43d verse. 'He brought forth his people with joy, and his chosen with gladness.' And who, my hearers, hath more need than ourselves to bring to remembrance this passage? Surely he hath brought us out 'with a mighty hand and a stretched–out arm.' And shall we not find the wilderness sweet, fed as we are with the manna of his grace? And is there not abundant cause to fill the vessels of our affections daily therewith? Yea, though God hath brought us out from among the horsemen and chariots of Pharaoh, though he hath sweetened the waters of Marah, and given us Elim wherein to encamp, yet may not the name of Jehovah be forgotten in the desert, as well as in Egypt? Yes, even in these days when heaven and earth are trembling at the voice of Almighty wrath, I fear there are many drowsy souls among us. Oh, awaken, I pray you; lest Satan have a commission from God to rock you, and you be lost forever! It is fearful to think how you may fall asleep on the brinkof a precipice, and dream that you are created a king, and guarded with a goodly train of ancient nobles, and stately palaces, and enriched with the revenues, majesty, and magnificence of a mighty kingdom,—and after all, the thunder of divine vengeance may sound in your ears, and starting up at the terrible noise thereof, you may fall into the raging sea of fire which burneth forever. There must be no halt, between christians among us. We must be zealous. But look unto thine heart, set a watch over thy tongue, beware of wildfire in thy zeal. There is much need of this caution in these days, when tongue is sharpened against tongue, and pen poisoned against pen, and pamphlets come out with more teeth to bite, than arguments to convince. This is but to betray the truth, and do the devil's service under God's colors. There are some among us, (and he looked full upon Brown, as he spoke,) who are violent and impatient in matters of religion,—given to vain forms, and traditions of men; adhering with a blind, pertinacious zeal to the customs of their progenitors. Of such I would have you beware. Nor would I have you roaming about, giving your ear to every new doctrine. Liberty of conscience is the gilded bait whereby Satan has caught many souls. The threshold of hell is paved with toleration. Leave hidden matters with God, and difficult texts of scripture with the elders of the church. I cannot, if I would, tell you the value of a godly, exemplary ministry among you. May we prove to you 'a savour of life unto life, and not of death unto death.' God, in his mercy, hath brought us out of England, which I fear is becoming sadly degenerate, and planted us among his heritage here; and the first use I would make of the office wherewithal I am honored, is to say to you, talk little about religion, and feel much of its power. Follow the light which is givenyou. 'Commune with your own heart, and be still.' Be constantly preparing something for others to copy. 'Nulla dies sine lineâ.' The more of heaven there is seen in your daily deportment, the more is God glorified. Carry yourselves as if your business was with eternity, your trade and traffic there; like the citiizens of the New Jerusalem, 'having your conversation in heaven, looking for the coming of the Lord Jesus Christ.' But what shall I say to you who have lusts too strong for your light, and corruption too strong for your convictions,—who go to hell just by heaven? I do humbly hope that I may so discharge the duties of mine office, that my hands may be washed of your damnation. But I beseech you to think in time. Consider if all your idle talk and wicked thoughts were written, what volumes of vanity and blasphemy it would make. However, angels take note, and conscience books them all. As for you who are careless and profane among us, who had rather dance round the May–pole of Morton, bedecked with ribbons and lascivious verses, than be hearing the wholesome and lion–like truths of the gospel,—you might laugh at me, were I to charge you not to meet me out of Christ; but I do charge you not to do it, and let him laugh who wins."

As Mr. Higginson drew toward the close of his discourse, shadows were noticed on the sunny threshold of the meetinghouse, and the honorable gentlemen from Plymouth walked in, and took their seats beside the speaker. The charge was given by elder Brewster, in which he principally dwelt on the awful responsibilities of his office, and the high honor Christ had done them, in sending them forth as laborers in his vineyard. Governor Bradford gave the right hand of fellowship with the dignified formality which was said to characterize him on public occasions.

"Well, what do you think of the sermon?" said Mr. Conant, as they mingled with the departing throng.

"Why, I think his tongue will never owe his mouth a penny's rent, if he never preaches such another," answered Mr. Oldham. "I trow that any godly man would be willing to lend his ears, scotfree, to such a sermon as that, seven days out of a week."

"I am suspicious some ears did not receive it very well," quoth another. "Didn't you see that Brown and his seditious company were vexed therewithal?"

"It's wosome to think," rejoined Mr. Oldham, "that there will so soon be difficulties among us. Here is Mr. Brown, now, whom I take to be a very comely sort of a personage in other respects, encouraging his people to chew the ratsbane of Satan, in that he privately readeth unto them the book of common prayer."

"Those were very savory words, which Mr. Higginson addressed to him," observed Mr. Conant. "I marvel that the Lord doth not send forth his javelin, and hurry such fellows from the earth."

"He is not given, like some people that I know of, to the abominable heresy of falling off from grace," interrupted Mr. Graves; "and he seemeth not to meddle with other people's matters."

"I tell you," returned Mr. Conant, "that whosoever is willing to tolerate any false religion, or discrepant way of religion, that his own may be tolerated, will for a need hang God's Bible on the devil's girdle. And as for other people's matters, I should like to know if God's glory is other people's matters;—and therefore to be given into the hands of the heathen and the papist? I should like to have Mr. Higginson hear such like sentiments."

"It is a small matter to me who heareth my sentiments," replied Mr. Graves; "forasmuch as I and mypeople are about to remove to Shawmut. They say the shipping hath far access into the land in that place; and that the woods are well stored with white oak, not a jot below our English timber."

"A new broom sweepeth clean," answered Mr. Conant; "but there is one thing I can tell you,—ours wore to a stub very quick. The Lord's work will go on at a grand rate, carried on as it is by a race of wandering Jacobites, taking dislike at every little difficulty. The ploughable plains, forsooth, are too dry and sandy for them; and the rocky places, although more fruitful, yet to eat their bread with toil of hand, they deem it insupportable; and so away they hie to their new possessions. I tell you, Mr. Graves, bad as you found us, you know nothing at all, as it were, of the terrors of a new plantation."

"I think I have had some occasion to remember sickness and hard labor, though I have known but little concerning scarcity of bread," replied the man of dolorous countenance. "But though the Lord putteth his people to some trials, he upholdeth them in time of danger, and comforteth them in time of need. After all, it maketh but little difference what part of this wilderness a man chooseth. It all seems dismal enough to a body from the old countries."

"Yes," rejoined Mr. Oldham. "I often think of what a witty man at Plymouth once said. Quoth he, 'it may be said of the two Englands, as our Saviour said of the wine, "no man having tasted the old straightway desireth the new; for he saith the old is better."

All this while, Mary, who had taken a cross path with Mr. and Mrs. Collier, found means to linger behind, and hear many kind things from Brown. It was likewise observed, that

Hopkins dined with his rival; although, as some said, Sally's eyes sparkled with malicious exultation when his stentorian voice was heard far out of time and tune in his favorite Old Hundred. Buildings were not numerous enough to give shelter to all their visitors; so tents were erected in the fields, and the multitude were furnished with provisions, plentiful enough, though coarse, and homely in the preparation.

Various were the discussions which were held that day. Some sat apart and talked of state policy, in dark hints and mysterious insinuations; while others loudly and boldly deprecated the high–handed course of the second Stuart. Some dwelt on the great goodness of God in raising them up from their low estate, to the enjoyment of outward comfort, and gospel privileges; or entered into theological controversies, in which a penetrating eye might discover the embryo forms of Familism, Gortonism, and divers other long forgotten sects, which in their day and generation had a reason for the faith that was in them. Many a rough, untutored swain paid his blunt compliments to a rosy cheek, and many a ruddy damsel "whispered, in biblical phrase, her soft words of encouragement and welcome."

CHAP. X.

Their judge was conscience, and her rule their law.
   — Cowper

Men so entirely uncongenial as Brown and his companions could not long tolerate each other. To the talents and virtues of many of them he gave a voluntary tribute of respect and admiration; but some ofthem were so far below his intellectual standard, that nothing could have saved them from his contempt, save the strong bond of religious unity; and under no circumstances, and in no situation whatever, could Brown have been a Puritan. Perhaps he and his adversaries equally mistook the pride of human opinion, for conscientious zeal; but their contradictory sentiments owed their origin to native difference of character. Spiritual light, like that of the natural sun, shines from one source, and shines alike upon all; but it is reflected and absorbed in almost infinite variety; and in the moral, as well as the natural world, the diversity of the rays is occasioned by the nature of the recipient.

Brown had gradually grown more daring in the declaration of his belief; but it was not until the Sabbath after ordination that he publicly evinced his adherence to the rites of the

Episcopal church. A meeting was held in a vacant building which had been erected as a common house until more convenient dwellings could be procured. Here a considerable number were collected; and the English ritual was read, and the sacrament administered by Mr. Blackstone in his full, canonical robes, according to the ceremonies prescribed by James and his Bishops at the council of Hampton House.

This was a thing not to be passed over. Mr. Blackstone living alone in his solitary hut at Tri–Mountain, was out of their jurisdiction; but Brown and his brother were the next morning ordered to appear before an assembly of the elders, to answer the charges brought against them. At 4 o'clock in the afternoon the inhabitants of Salem were seen again collecting at their meetinghouse to hear what could be said in defence of the culprits.

After a suitable pause, the Governor arose, as he said, "You Mr. Charles and Samuel Brown are accused of fomenting disturbance among the people, forasmuch as you have taught them that under the shadow of the mitre is the only place where men ought to worship. Do you plead guilty thereto?"

"That I bow with reverence before the holy mitre, is most true, Governor Endicott; but in no respect whatever have I bred disturbance among the people."

"Have you not," interrupted Mr. Conant, "have you not made them drink of the wine of Babylon? Yea, have you not made them drunk with her fornication? Have you not, like the red dragon, pursued the church into the wilderness, and poured out a flood after her, that you might cause her to be destroyed?"

"My answers are to Governor Endicott, and the elders of what you term the church," replied Brown, with respectful coldness.

"Mr. Conant," said the Governor, "these things should be done decently, and in order. It is the business of men in authority to inquire into this matter. Have you, young man, upheld the ritual of the first–born daughter of the church of Rome, and maintained that the arm of royal authority ought to enforce obedience thereto?"

"I have said," replied Brown, "that 'Religio docenda est, non coercenda,' was a bad maxim of state policy; and that 'Hæresis dedocenda est, non permittenda,' was a far

61

better. If by the first—born daughter of Rome, you mean that church descended in a direct line from Jesus Christ and his Apostles, a church at the feet of which the most sacred and virtuous Elizabeth bowed down her majestic head, and beneath the shelter of whose mighty arm the learned king James, and our liege prince Charles, have reposedtheir triple diadem—if you mean this church, I do say, her sublime ritual should be enforced, till every fibre of the king's dominions yields a response thereto. Saints have worn her white robe, and her mitre has rested on holy men. The sacred water hath been on my unworthy head, and therewithal have their hands signed the mystic symbol of redemption. And I would rather," continued he, raising the tones of his fine, manly voice, "I would rather give my limbs to the wolves of your desert, than see her sceptre broken by men like yourselves."

"Think you," said Governor Endicott, smiling, "that king James cared aught for the church, save that he considered it the basis of the throne? You forget his open declaration in the assembly at Edinburgh. 'The church of Geneva,' saith he, 'keepeth pasche and yule; what have they for them? They have no institution. As for our neighbour kirk of England, their service is an evil said mass in English. They want none of the mass but the liftings.' "

"King James had not then come to the English throne," answered Brown. "He found cause to alter his opinion after he had felt the blessed influence of that church, and seen many of her corner stones, elect and precious."

"Nay, Mr. Brown," rejoined the Governor, "there is enow wherewithal to convince your reason, for you are not wanting in the light which leadeth astray, that it was 'king craft,' which made James turn his back upon a church whereunto he had given the name of the 'sincerest kirk in the whole world;' and, with all reverence to his royal memory, I cannot but think that his love of forms and ceremonies was but a taint of hereditary evil from his Moabitish mother. Forasmuch as I am a loyal subject of king Charles, it is neither wise nor safe for me to find specks and blemishesin his government; but to my thinking, there is but a fine—spun thread between the crosier and the liturgy, the embroidered mantle and the bishop's gown; and who does not know that the heart of the king is fastened to the rosary of Henrietta Maria? And that the mummeries of Rome are, at her instigation, heard within the palace of St. James? But after all, Mr. Brown, there is one higher than princes. It was a cardinal truth, which Cardinal Pole spake unto Henry the Eighth, 'Penes reges inferre bellum, penes autem Deum terminare.' "

"And I marvel that men of sense, like yourself, Governor Endicott, can expect the sword of the Lord to be quiet in its scabbard, when the robe of religion is torn, and her altars overturned," replied Brown; "and that too, by men unto whom you give your countenance—a parcel of separatists and anabaptists, covering their sins with the cloak of religion, and concealing their own factious and turbulent spirit there–with."

Upon this Mr. Higginson and Mr. Skelton arose and made answer:

"Neither as factious men affecting a popular parity in the church, nor as schismatics aiming at the dissolution of the church ecclesiastical, but as faithful ministers of Christ, and liege subjects of king Charles, did we come hither. We have suffered much for nonconformity in our native land, and after much tribulation have we come to this place of liberty. Here the cap and the gown may not be urged upon us, for we consider these things as sinful abominations in the sight of God. So may the Almighty prosper us, as we have, in all humility, spoken the truth."

"Credat Judæus, non ego," replied Brown, scornfully. "It is easy to talk about conscience and humility, but wherein have you shown it, in that you judge the consciences of your brethren?"

"We have but testified against what we conceived to be the errors and abuses of the church," answered Mr. Higginson. "We have been made the humble instruments to begin the good work, which God will go on to perfect for his own praise and his people's. peace. Let good men sit still and behold his salvation. He that sitteth in the heavens, laugheth at the pride of men. The Most High hath them in derision; and their folly shall certainly be made known unto all."

"Mr. Brown," said the Governor, "you need not reply to this; for disrespectful words like unto those you have spoken, must not be repeated in my presence. Inasmuch as gentle means have been in vain used to convince you of your errors, it is our opinion that New England is no place for such haughty spirits to dwell within. Therefore, in the first vessel which departeth from these shores, we do order you to return from whence you came; and, in the meantime, we do command you to desist from convening the people together at any time; or in any wise calling their attention to common prayer."

"Let them that scorn the mitre, fear the crown," replied the angry young man. "Who is it that has wrought upon the minds of the people, persuading them that they should not march under the king's colors, pretending that his conscience is wounded by the popish sign of the cross, and thereby concealing his traitorous purposes against his sovereign? Mayhap you had spoken less freely within the court of St. James; but the sceptre can reach you even here, and you may yet tremble at its touch. There are those who can tell of your evil practices, and they shall be told in a voice of thunder."

So saying, the young man and his brother, with stately step, departed from the house.

"The council will sit some time longer," said Brown to his brother; "for they have other heretical matters to discuss. If you will give me notice when they begin to disperse, I will go directly to Mr. Conant's; for I must see Mary to-night."

"I could hardly stoop to woo the daughter of that dogmatical rascal," replied Samuel; "though I will acknowledge, she is the very queen of women."

"Pride can endure much in such a cause," rejoined his brother; "but I must away."

The young man sprung over the log enclosure, ran across a mendow to conceal his intended route from those within the dwelling, and in a few moments coming out into the open footpath, he hurried along with the rapid pace of a man in whose bosom painful thoughts are struggling and busy.

"Well," thought he, "I shall at least see England again—again tread on her classic ground, and gaze on her antique grandeur and cultivated beauty. But, oh, to leave her in such a place, is the bitterest thought of all. And what would be her lot, if far away from her, I should go to 'that bourne from whence no traveller returns?' "

But the heart of youth rebounds from the pressure of despondency—and presently brighter scenes were passing swiftly before him. One moment he was invested in the civil gown, the applause of princes and nobles resounding in his ears;—and the next presented Mary restored to her original rank, and shining amid the loveliest and proudest of the land. She too, had had many bitter thoughts; for she well knew the temper of the souls about her, and she felt that the decree of the assembly could not be otherwise than it had proved. When Brown entered, he received acordial grasp both from the mother and daughter, as they anxiously inquired,

"What have they done?"

"A vessel sails for England in a week," replied Brown; "and Samuel and I depart from America, perhaps forever."

Whenever Mary thought of the possibility of separation, and of late she had frequently feared that the time would soon come, she had felt that the youth was still dearer and dearer to her heart. And now when she heard him announce the speedy certainty of this, her pale lip quivered, and in the silent unreserve of hearts long wedded to each other, she threw herself sobbing on his neck, her slender arms clinging around him, in all the energy of grief.

"I know not," said Mrs. Conant, dashing the tears from her cheek, "I know not that I ought to allow this. Remember, dear Mary, what I owe to your father."

"Madam Conant," replied Brown, "we have loved each other too long, and too purely, to stand upon idle ceremonies at this painful moment. Had I been treated with more moderation, perhaps I might never have been so hasty as to declare my religious opinions. Then these unhappy differences had never arisen, and with my Mary, I could happily have shared a log hut in the wilderness. But I have been spurned, goaded, trampled on, as a heretic—and worse than all, I have been doomed to hear every thing blasphemed which I held most sacred. As it is, you cannot deny us this sorrowful alleviation of our lot."

"It is the duty of woman to love and obey her husband," answered Mrs. Conant; "but had you known whereunto my heart has been inclined in this matter—" she would have said more, but something unbidden rose and prevented her utterance.

"I do know it," rejoined the young man; "and wherever I go, you will be in my pleasantest and most grateful thoughts. But, Mary, it will not be always thus—You will come to England and be my wife."

Mary looked at her mother and sighed.

"It may as well be said as not, my child," observed Mrs. Conant. "I shall not long hang a dead weight upon your young life. Nay, do not weep, Mary; I know that you are willing to bear the burden, and that you have been kind and cheerful beneath it; but the shadows of life are fleeting more dimly before me, and I feel that I must soon be gathered to my fathers."

The expression brought with it a flash of painful recollection.

"No," continued she, "like the wife of Abraham, I must be buried far from my kindred. If my greyhaired father could but shed one tear upon my grave, methinks it would furnish wherewithal to cheer my drooping heart. I loved my husband,—nor have I ever repented that I followed him hither; but oh, Mary, I would not have you suffer as I have suffered, when I have thought of that solitary old man. 'The heart knoweth its own sorrows, and a stranger intermeddleth not with its grief.'"

"Dear mother," replied Mary, "you know that grandfather loves you, and has long since forgiven you. I have told you how often he used to take me in his lap and kiss me, as he said how much I looked like his dear child."

The mournful smile of consumption passed over the pale face of Mrs. Conant,—one of those smiles in which the glowing light of the etherial inhabitant seemed gleaming through its pale and broken tenement.

"Well, Mr. Brown," said she, "Mary will write a letter to her grandfather, and when you deliver it, give him therewith the duty and affection of his dying daughter. I could wish that Mary might be always with her father. He loves her, notwithstanding his conscientious scruples cause him to seem harsh; and perhaps she might feel happier when her days are numbered like mine. But I don't know—It is no doubt a painful sacrifice."

"Wherever I am," replied Brown, "my home shall be most gladly shared with Mary's father. Besides," continued he, smiling, "the prayer book should be hid, and not another word said about the surplice."

"I am glad to hear you speak so," interrupted Mary. "I was afraid you would be angry, inasmuch as I knew they would speak irreverently of our holy church."

"I was angry," answered Brown; "and I threatened that the king should be informed of heresy and treason."

"Oh, Charles, don't stir up their enemies in England," said Mary. "There are a great many good men among them; and I am sure they have difficulties enough already."

"I would not hurt a hair of their heads, if I could," rejoined her lover; "and sorry am I that my unruly tongue led me far beyond my reason in this matter. As you say, I believe some of them are conscientious; though the arch enemy of souls hath led them far from the true path of safety."

"I cannot think with you and Mary," observed Mrs. Conant, "about forms and ceremonies. But it appears to me that an error in judgment is nothing, if the life be right with God. I have lately thought that a humble heart was more than a strong mind, in perceiving the things appertaining to divine truth.Matters of dispute appear more and more like a vapor which passeth away. I have seldom joined in them; for it appears to me there is little good in being convinced, if we are not humbled; to know every thing about religion, and yet to feel little of its power— yea, even to feel burdened with a sense of sin and misery, and yet be content to remain in it."

"Why, I must say," replied Brown, "that I think the Bible is clear enough, as explained by our holy bishops. But to my mind, the view of God's works brings more devotion than any thing relating to controversy."

"Ah, Mr. Brown, the Bible is an inspired book; but I sometimes think the Almighty suffers it to be a flaming cherubim, turning every way, and guarding the tree of life from the touch of man. But in creation, one may read to their fill. It is God's library— the first Bible he ever wrote."

"Bless me," exclaimed Mary, "here is father at the very doors."

Her lover hastily relinquished her hand, and she sprang from his side; but there was no chance for him to retreat. Mrs. Conant's pulse throbbed high, for she saw that her husband was already in no pleasant humor. The old gentleman hung up his hat, and drew his chair forward, without being aware of the presence of any one but his own family, till Brown rose and stood before him. The countenance of Mr. Conant was flushed with anger, when he saw the bold intruder.

"Mr. Brown," said he, stamping his foot violently, "how came you hither?"

"Why, I came hither, you already know," replied the youth calmly; "and most gladly would I have had my last visit here, a peaceable one."

The tyrannical man opened the door, and pointed to it, as he said, "A man may not touch pitch, and remain undefiled. I marvel if you bring not a curse on the whole house."

"I was about to depart," answered his guest; "but there is one thing I would say before I go. In my anger I spoke disrespectfully to men older and better than myself. It is a matter of choice as well as of necessity to leave New England, and be no more among you; and now, Mr. Conant, for the sake of those who are dear to me, I would fain have our parting, not that of churchman and non−conformist, but of christians."

"Out with you, and your damnable doctrines, you hypocritical son of a strange woman," exclaimed Mr. Conant.

Pride was struggling hard for utterance, as Brown moved towards the door; but for Mary's sake it was repressed—and before the old man was aware of his purpose, he stept back and took the hand of the mother and daughter, as he said,

"God bless you both. To me you have been all kindness."

He then made a formal, stately bow to Mr. Conant, who muttered,

"Take my curse with you," and slammed the door after him.

Mary rushed into her apartment, and hiding her face in the bed clothes, gave free vent to her tears.

But the poor may not long indulge their grief. Her father's supper must be prepared, and her mother's wants must not be neglected; and, with as much serenity as she could assume, she again appeared in his presence. The tears of his sickly wife had allayed the first gust of passion, and perhaps even the heart of that rigid man reproached him for its violence. Howeverthat might be, pride would suffer no symptoms of remorse to appear before his family. Every thing went wrong through the whole evening. The cake was burned,—and the milk was not sweet,—and there had been too much fire to prepare their little repast; till wearied out with his continual fretfulness, they both retired to their beds at an early hour, and Mary sobbed herself into an uneasy slumber.

(*)CHAP. XI.

```
        Farewell!
Oh, in that word—that fatal word—howe'er
We promise—hope—believe—there breathes despair.
    — Byron
```

The interim between Brown's sentence and his departure, seemed like "a hideous dream." In vain Mary tried to recognize its certainty enough to prepare the letter which he was to convey. It was not until the day before the dreaded event, that the solicitations of her mother prevailed on her to commence the task; and when she did, the pen remained uplifted, and the stainless sheet lay for a long time before her, while she pressed her hand upon her brow in a bewilderment of misery. She wrote "Deare Grandfather,"— but could proceed no further. The name of that fond, doting relation was encircled with painful thoughts. By him she had been reared with more than tenderness, like some fair and slender blossom in his gardens. There she had been the little idol ofthe brilliant circle. There too, she had first seen Charles Brown, and mingled with him in the graceful evolutions of the dance, while her young heart in vain strove to be proof against the intoxicating witchery of light and motion. And there, as she gazed on his lofty forehead, stamped with the proud, deep impress of intellect, and watched the changeful lustre of his dark, eloquent eyes, that alternately beamed with high or tender thoughts, she too became covetous of mental riches, and worshipped at the shrine of genius. Amid this fairy dream, the stern voice of duty was heard commanding her to depart from her country and her kindred, and to go to a land of strangers. It recks not how many sighs and tears it cost, the sacrifice was made; and Heaven in reward gave to her solitude the only being that could enliven its dreariness.

What was she now? A lily weighed down by the pitiless pelting of the storm; a violet shedding its soft, rich perfume on bleakness and desolation; a plant which had been fostered and cherished with mild sunshine and gentle dews, removed at once from the hot–house to the desert, and left to unfold its delicate leaves beneath the darkness of the lowering storm. And of the two, for whom she had cheerfully endured this change, one was already within sight of the mansions of the blest—and the other was soon to be like a bright and departed vision. 'Twas bitterness, all bitterness, and she bowed down her head and wept.

"It must not be thus," said she, as she thoughtfully walked across the room. The painful sacrifice was made with serenity; and none shall say, that I at last shrunk from the trial—" and with steadier nerve, she wrote as follows:

"Deare Grandfather,

"I againe take up my penn to write upon the same paper you gave me when I left you, and tolde me thereupon to write my thoughts in the deserte. Alas, what few I have, are sad ones. I remember you once saide that Shakspeare would have beene the same greate poet if he had been nurtured in a Puritan wildernesse. But indeed it is harde for incense to rise in a colde, heavy atmosphere, or for the buds of fancie to put forth, where the heartes of men are as harde and sterile as their unploughed soile. You will wonder to hear me complain, who have heretofore beene so proud of my cheerfulnesse. Alas, howe often is pride the cause of things whereunto we give a better name. Perhaps I have trusted too muche to my owne strengthe in this matter, and Heaven is nowe pleased to send a more bitter dispensation, wherewithal to convince me of my weakness. I woulde tell you more, venerable parente, but Mr. Brown will conveye this to your hande, and he will saye much, that I cannot finde hearte or roome for. The settlement of this Western Worlde seemeth to goe on fast now that soe many men of greate wisdome and antient blood are employed therein. They saye much concerning our holie church being the Babylone of olde, and that vials of fierce wrath are readie to be poured out upon her. If the prophecies of these mistaken men are to be fulfilled, God grante I be not on earthe to witnesse it. My dear mother is wasting awaye, though I hope she will long live to comforte me. She hath often spoken of you lately. A fewe dayes agone, she said she shoulde die happier if her grey–haired father coulde shed a tear upon her grave. I well know that when that daye does come, we shall both shed many bitter tears. I must leave some space in this paper for her feeble hande to fill. The Lord have you inHis holie keeping till your dutifull grandchilde is againe blessed with the sighte of your countenance.

"With all love and reverence,

70

"Your Affectionate and Dutifull Childe, "Mary Conant."

"Deare and Venerable Sire,

"I knowe nott wherewithal to address you, for my hearte is full, and my hande trembleth with weaknesse. My kinde Mary is mistaken in thinking I shall long sojourne upon Earthe. I see the grave opening before me, but I feel that I cannot descend thereunto till I have humbly on my knees asked the forgiveness of my offended father. He who hath made man's hearte to suffer, alone knoweth the wretchedness of mine when I have thought of your solitary old age. Pardon, I beseech you, my youthfull follie and disobedience, and doe not take offence if I write that the husbande for whose sake I have suffered much, hath been through life a kinde and tender helpe–meete; for I knowe it will comforte you to think upon this, when I am dead and gone. I would saye much more, but though my soule is strong in affection for you, my body is weake. God Almighty bless you, is the prayer of

"Your loving Daughtere, "Mary Conant."

The letter once finished, how was it to be delivered to the young man? Mr. Conant had given commands which his wife dared not disobey, and seemed more than ever inclined to keep watch upon Mary's motions. In this dilemma she resolved to tax the ready wit of her friend Sally; but when she sought Mrs. Collier for that purpose, she found her ready equipped for a journey.

"What, are you going to Plymouth so soon?" asked Mary. "I thought you told me you did go not till to–morrow."

"And so I supposed then," answered Sally; "but John hath heard that the boat will sail this afternoon, and he is coming for me shortly. I was just stepping in, to bid you good–bye."

"And you are going away from Salem then, for— always," said Mary, as the tears came to her eyes. "What shall I do, when you are gone?"

"You used to tell me to trust in God," replied her friend, "and perhaps I did wrong that I did not think more of such sober talk. I declare, I did not suppose any thing would have made me so sorry to go back to Plymouth," added she, and the ready tears of sympathy trickled down her cheeks.

"Well, good—bye," said Mary, as she threw her arms round her neck in the full tide of girlish affection. "I shall always love you for your kindness to me and my good mother. Peradventure when we are both ancient women, there will be a road cut through from hence, and I shall come and see you."

At another time Mary would have mourned bitterly over the loss of her old associate; but now in the selfishness of more weighty sorrows, she hardly expended a thought upon it. Her whole mind was occupied in devising a method of seeing Brown, free from interruption. We know that love now usually finds means to effect his purpose, and it seems he laughed as loudly at locksmiths in 1629, as he does in these degenerate days. At the instigation of Mr. Brown, the widow Willet (whose red cardinal gave such offence to Mr. Oldham), was induced to request Mary's company through the night, under pretence of her son's absence. The lonely woman had frequently asked the same favor, and it was, of course, granted withouthesitation. Once arrived within her dwelling, the sorrowful young couple were left to an undisturbed discourse upon their present prospects and future plans. The night passed rapidly away, and the sun rose brightly on the pale and agitated pair, as if no hearts were there, to meet his rays with sickening desolation. Brown rested his arm upon Mary's shoulder, and pointed to the rising light, as he said,

"It is the signal of separation. The vessel sails at early sunrise. Would it had never been day."

"Oh," replied Mary, "were it not for the hope of speedy re—union, how gladly would I now lay down my aching head deep, deep, in the cold earth."

"Talk not so sadly, Mary," answered her lover. "If your mother lives long, I shall again come to America, at least for a season; and if she dies, you will soon return to your grandfather, who will make us both happy."

"Alas, Charles," replied she, "it makes me shudder to think of the wickedness of such devoted love. I did even wish to night that mother's earthly trials were all over, and I at liberty to follow you wheresoever you went, through storms or sunshine. It was a wicked thought, and I struggled till I overcame it."

"Be ever thus, my own dear girl," rejoined the young man. "I could not love you if you were otherwise. May the atmosphere of your mind be always so pure that a passing cloud has power wherewithal to disturb it."

For some moments he stood silently clasping her to his heart. He moved from her, and made a reluctant motion toward the table where he had placed his hat—walked across the room again and again—looked out upon the increasing light, and cursed its swiftness; at length, a loud, shrill blast came upon the morning air; "'Tis the last signal for all to be on board," exclaimed he; "and now I must depart."

She sprung to his embrace, and his arms twined round her, "and clung as they would cling forever." One deep, painful pause, one fervent, long protracted kiss on that cold brow, and he was gone.

The maiden slowly returned to her father's house, sick, exhausted, and weary of life. The household duties were silently and serenely performed; and no outward token of anguish could be discovered save a death-like paleness. Two hours elapsed, and yet the gay pennon of the Queen Elizabeth was seen fluttering in the air. Mary could not follow the multitude to the beach, and give the sacredness of her grief to the vulgar gaze; but she sought a woody, retired hill, and watched the departure of her lover's vessel, which with spreading sails, was soon seen wheeling from the shore. A handkerchief was waving from the quarter deck; it was a farewell signal, and was speedily answered. It again waved toward the thicket, and Mary knew that her last token of love had not passed unobserved. Her intense and eager gaze was never turned from the object, until the red-cross flag indistinctly mingled with the horizon. Mary looked on the bright, blue expanse of water before her. The deep furrows, which had so lately marred its beauty, had all passed away, as suddenly as the tribulations of boyhood; and as she turned away from that smooth surface, she, for the first time, realized what she had as yet shrunk from acknowledging, the cheerless, utter solitude of the heart.

CHAP. XII.

Erewhile, where yon gay spires their brightness rear,
Trees waved, and the brown hunter's shouts were loud
Amid the forest; and the bounding deer
Fled at the glancing plume, and the gaunt wolf yelled near.

Hobomok

— Bryant

During the long and dreary winter which followed, there was nothing to break the monotony of the scene, except the occasional visits of Hobomok, who used frequently to come up from Plymouth and join the hunters in their excursions. At such seasons, he was all vigor and elasticity; and none returned more heavily laden with furs and venison, than the tawny chieftain. The best of these spoils were always presented to the "child of the Good Spirit," as he used to call Mary; and never to Squantam or Abbamocho had he paid such unlimited reverence.

A woman's heart loves the flattery of devoted attention, let it come from what source it may. Perhaps Mary smiled too complacently on such offerings; perhaps she listened with too much interest, to descriptions of the Indian nations, glowing as they were in the brief, figurative language of nature. Be that as it may, love for Conant's daughter, love deep and intense, had sunk far into the bosom of the savage. In minds of a light and thoughtless cast, love spreads its thin, fibrous roots upon the surface, and withers when laid open to the scorching trials of life; but in souls of sterner mould, it takes a slower and deeper root. The untutored chief knew not the strange visitant which had usurped such empire in his heart; ifhe found himself gazing upon her face in silent eagerness, 'twas but adoration for so bright an emanation from the Good Spirit; if something within taught him to copy, with promptitude, all the kind attentions of the white man, 'twas gratitude for the life of his mother which she had preserved. However, female penetration knew the plant, though thriving in so wild a soil; and female vanity sinfully indulged its growth. Sometimes a shuddering superstition would come over her, when she thought of his sudden appearance in the mystic circle, and she would sigh at the vast distance which separated her from her lover; but the probability of Brown's return, would speedily chase away such thoughts.

Hobomok seldom spoke in Mr. Conant's presence, save in reply to his questions. He understood little of the dark divinity which he attempted to teach, and could not comprehend wherein the traditions of his fathers were heathenish and sinful; but with Mary and her mother, he felt no such restraint, and there he was all eloquence.

It was in the middle of the "cold moon," by which name he used to designate January, that he arrived in Salem, on one of his numerous visits, bringing with him some skins of the beautiful grey fox of the Mississippi.

Hobomok

"Hobomok brought you fur for moccassins," said he, as he handed them to Mary.

"How very soft it is," said she, showing it to her mother. "It seems like the handsome fur, which grandfather had from Russia. You did not kill it yourself, Hobomok?"

The Indian shook his head. "His tracks are toward the setting sun," replied he. "Hobomok give beaver skins like sand to a warrior come in from the west. He say they call it Muzaham Shungush.There is a council–fire at Mount Haup. The chiefs think the hunter came not to trade for beaver skins, but to find how heavy the red men of Ossamequin, Sassacus, Miantonimo, and Uncas."

"Have none of them been hither, heretofore?" inquired Mary.

"One warrior came among us in the moon of flowers,* and spread his blanket with us through the hunting moon. I talked with him, like as with the Yengees. He told big stories about his tribe; but he say Great Spirit lay between us, and his back bone so high, make foot of the Indian weary. The chiefs said he counted red men then; but the cloud passed over."

"Well," rejoined Mary, "I hope they'll bring more such handsome fur hither. If they come to count the red men, peradventure they'll find them too heavy. You see I am going to make you a wampum belt of the shells you brought, and I want you to tell me how to put them together."

"Hobomok glad," replied the Indian, his eyes sparkling with joy at such a proof of gratitude. "You see that shell, the color of the sky when the sun goes down? Put him in the big moose there," pointing to the middle of the belt. "Him like the rainbow, put on the back of the deer; and him like the heaped snow, put on the big snake. That's like Tatobam's wampum. Tatobam kill snakes—make great spirit snake very angry—That's reason the Indian from the west call him Tongoomlishcah."

"And who is he?" asked Mary.

"The grass has now grown on Tatobam's grave, and trees are planted thereon," answered the savage. "He was the father of Sassacus, great Sachem of the Pequods. In council, cunning as the beaver, and quick–sightedas the eagle. His tribe were like swallows before a storm, and his wrath like the rising of a thunder cloud. Furious as a wounded buffalo in the fight, but true to his love as the star of the north."

"And was she good enough for so great a warrior?" rejoined Mary.

"His Mohegan squaw was bright and handsome as the wakon–bird of the west. Her voice cheered the sachem, like the song of the muck–a–wiss, that tells of frost gone by. In the dance she was nimble as the deer, and quick as the diving loon. But the quiver of Mohegan was sent to the Pequod, and it was wound with the skin of the snake."

"And then he made war upon his squaw's tribe, I suppose?"

"Tatobam's men were thick as leaves in autumn, his quiver was full, his bow was strong, and his arrow sharp as the lightning, when the Great Spirit sends it forth in his anger. There would have been few left among the Mohegans to black their faces for the dead. The voice of his tribe was for battle. The hunter heard their war–song far away in the desert, like the notes of the woodpecker, which tell of the tempest. So the council–fire was extinguished. The face of Tatobam was anointed, and his belt buckled for the fight. But Indian can love," said he, as he stooped low, and looked up in Mary's face.

"How did Tatobam prove it?" inquired Mrs. Conant.

"Grass never grows in the war–path of the Pequod. His warriors said they would bring home the scalps of their enemies before the rising of the sun. They called on Tatobam to lead to the fight, that they might drink the blood of Mohegan. Before the moon went behind the hills, his tracks were upon the sand; the rising tide washed them away. He rose up atthe call of his tribe, and they knew not he had been forth alone. They found not a sleeping enemy. The ambush of the Pequod was broken. The tomahawk was changed for the peace pipe, and the marriage dance was seen in the wigwam of Tatobam."

"Hobomok," interrupted Mr. Conant, who entered at this moment, "it is a pity you were not out with your bow, forasmuch as a fine deer just ran through the settlement."

"There's a tribe of 'em, out on the plains to night," answered the Indian. "Their tracks are thick as flies in the Sturgeon moon.* Sagamore John's men are coming out with—with—" and unable to think of the English word, he pointed to the candle.

"Oh, they are coming out by torch–light," exclaimed Mary, "as Hobomok says the western Indians do. How I do wish I could see them hunt by torch–light."

"I shall go out with you," said Mr. Conant, "to see what success the Lord giveth us in this matter. I have heard wonderful stories appertaining to the taking of deer after this fashion. They say that in the lightest night that ever was made, the creatures are so bewitched, that they'll not move a jot, after they once get sight of the fire."

"And wherefore shouldn't I go, father?" asked Mary.

"A pretty sight truly," replied the old man, "to see you out at midnight with twenty hunters."

"But," rejoined his wife, "two or three horses can be procured; and if a few of the young folks will go, assuredly I see no harm therein; more especially as you will accompany Mary. You must remember," continued she, in an insinuating tone, "that there are few such like gratifications in this wilderness."

"No doubt there is enough of them; wherewithal to entice their wandering hearts," answered her husband; "but if you think it fitting the girl should go, verily I have no objection thereto."

Preparations were accordingly made. The window Willet agreed to come up and stay with Mrs. Conant; and a few young women readily consented to accompany Mary, on such horses as the settlement could afford. As for Hobomok, he was all eagerness to display his skill. His arrows were carefully selected, and the strength of his bow was tried again and again, as he occasionally turned to Mary, and boasted of the service it had always done him, in field and forest.

Winter seldom presents a night of such glittering beauty, as the one they chose for their expedition. The mellow light of moon and star looked down upon the woods, and as the trees danced to the shrill music of the winds, their light was reflected by ten thousand undulating motions, in all the rich varieties of frost work. It seemed as if the sylphs and fairies, with which imagination of old, peopled the mountain and the stream, had all assembled to lay their diamond offerings on the great altar of nature. Silently Mary gazed on the going down of that bright planet, and tree and shrub bowed low their spangled plumes in homage to her retiring majesty, till her oblique rays were only to be seen in faint and scattered radiance, on the cold, smooth surface of the earth.

At length the party were in motion, proceeding through the woods by the twinkling lustre of the stars. Mr. Conant held the rein of Mary's horse, and guided his footsteps along the rough and narrow path. Hobomok walked by her side, as silent and thoughtful as he usually was in the presence of her father. They soon came out upon the open plain; and a few momentsafter, six neighboring Indians were seen winding along from the opposite woods, with their torches carried upon poles high above their heads, casting their lurid glare on the mild, tranquil light of the evening. As they drew up, a few inquiries were made by Hobomok in his native tongue, and answered by his companions in scarcely an audible tone, as they significantly placed their fingers upon their lips. Mr. Conant and his ten associates formed a line and fell into the rear, while the Indians who carried the poles, did the same, and placed themselves forward. It was indeed a strange, romantic scene. The torches sent up columns of dense, black smoke, which vainly endeavoured to rise in the clear, cold atmosphere. Hobomok stood among his brethren, gracefully leaning on his bow, and his figure might well have been mistaken for the fabled deity of the chase. The wild, fitful light shone full upon the unmoved countenance of the savage, and streamed back unbroken upon the rigid features of the Calvinist, rendered even more dark in their expression by the beaver cap which deeply shaded his care-worn brow. The pale loveliness of Mary's face, amid the intense cold of the night, seemed almost as blooming as her ruddy companions; and the frozen beauty of the surrounding woods again flashed brightly beneath the unwonted glow of those artificial rays.

There, in that little group, standing in the loneliness and solitude of nature, was the contrast of heathen and christian, social and savage, elegance and strength, fierceness and timidity. Every eye bent forward, and no sound broke in upon the stillness, excepting now and then, the low, dismal growl of the wolf was heard in the distance. Whenever this fearful sound came upon the ear, the girls would involuntarily move nearer to their protectors, who repeatedlyassured them that wolves would never approach a fire. Presently a quick, light step was heard, and a deer glided before them. The beautiful animal, with rapid and graceful motion, was fast hurrying to the woods, when his eye seemed caught by the singular light which gleamed around him. He paused, and looking back, turned his pert, inquiring gaze full upon the hunters. He saw the forms of men, and knew they were his enemies; but so powerful was the fascination of the torches, that his majestic antlers seemed motionless as the adjacent shrubbery.

78

The arrow of Hobomok was already drawn to the head, when Mary touched his shoulder, as she said, "Don't kill it, Hobomok—don't;" but the weapon was already on the wing, and from his hand it seldom missed its mark. The deer sprung high into the air, its beautiful white breast was displayed for an instant, a faint, mournful sound was heard—and Hobomok stept forward to seize the victim he had wounded. As he brought it up to Mary, the glossy brown of its slender sides was heaving with the last agonies of life, and she turned away from the painful sight.

But a short space ensued, ere another was seen sweeping across the plain. He too noticed the unnatural brightness, and stood bound by the same bewitching spell. One of the Indians gave his torch to Hobomok, and placing his eye on a level with his bow, took steady and deliberate aim. However, it seemed he had not effected his purpose entirely; for the creature uttered a piercing cry, and bounded forward with incredible swiftness. The next Indian handed his torch to one of the white men, and rushing before his companion, he buried his knife deep in the bosom of the wounded deer. A loud laugh of derision followed.

"It's mine," exclaimed he, in Indian language, "It's mine, for I killed it."

"'Tisn't yours," retorted the other, furiously; "the deer hadn't run ten rods; and a hunter never gave up a beast under that."

The girls could not understand what was spoken by the contending savages; but they saw that a quarrel was likely to ensue, and Mary whispered to her father to guide them homeward. The route they had taken was a short one, and the difficulties in retracing it were few. The maidens gladly welcomed their own quiet apartments, and Mr. Conant returned to the plain. The Indian who had first wounded the animal, had proudly relinquished his claim, and stood by, in sullen, offended majesty. The others were preparing a new set of flambeaux for a fresh attack.

CHAP. XIII.

Strong was the love to heaven, which bare
From their dear homes and altars far,
The old, the young, the wise, the brave,
The rich, the noble, and the fair,

Hobomok

And led them o'er the mighty wave,
Uncertain peril's front to dare.
   — Yamoyden

Notwithstanding the occasional excitements which we have mentioned, the winter passed wearily away; and to Mary, the moral as well as the natural atmosphere, was chill and heavy. The earth, in this cold, northern climate, wore one uniform robe of state— her spotless ermine, studded with jewels. Even in this dress, she displayed much to excite a poetic imagination and a devotional heart; but the souls of men were not open to the influence of nature. Little thought they, amid the fierce contests of opinion, of the latent treasures of mind or the rich sympathies of taste. Still, their stern piety was lofty and genuine, though deeply colored with the ignorance and superstition of the times. A sound, doctrinal exposition of Romans brought more religious warmth into their hearts, than the nightly exhibition of the numerous hosts shining in the broad belt of the heavens, those mighty apostles, which God has sent forth to proclaim throughout creation, his majesty and power. Mary grew more and more weary of the loneliness of unreciprocated intellect; and when she thought of Brown, it seemed as if winter would never depart. But though the wings of time appeared clogged, and folded about him in heaviness, he wheeled the same course through the sky; and Spring was soon seen peeping from the sunny gates of heaven, and strewing her wild–flower wreath along the woods.

Intelligence had reached New England that a large company of godly brethren were coming out early in the season, among whom was Mrs. Johnson, the favorite sister of the Earl of Lincoln. Mary had known the lady Arabella in Lincolnshire, and she now kept an almost constant watch upon the seashore, in the eager anticipation of meeting with her friend. Perhaps even that friend was frequently forgotten in the thoughts of one still dearer; for she had heard nothing from Brown since his departure, and her heart grew sick with "hope deferred."

It was late in May, when, as she was walking by the seashore, gazing on the bright scene, to her so painfully associated, she espied two vessels under fullsail, and her spirits danced with the certainty of intelligence from her lover, if not his actual presence. The news was hastily communicated, and all felt disappointed when they were discovered to be under foreign colors. The suspicion at once arose that they were Dunkirkers, and, of course, enemies to the English. The alarm was given, and every man seized his loaded gun, and prepared to give them a hostile reception. Luckily, however, the precaution was found unnecessary. The ships rode quietly into port, and proved to be merchantmen from the Netherlands, bringing a large supply of provisions and utensils of various kinds, to exchange for beaver skins. Another fortnight passed slowly away, and it was rumored that one of the Arabella company had safely arrived at Shawmut; but still there came no intelligence to hush the tumult of Mary's hopes and fears. At length, on the 12th of June 1630, the settlers had scarcely swung their axes over their shoulders, or fastened the plough to their oxen, at early sunrise, before the tall mast of the Arabella was seen careering above the waves, bending her prow, and "walking the waters like a thing of life." And as she came within hearing, the cheerful note of the trumpet, proclaiming, "Capt. Millburn of the Arabella—sixty-five days from Yarmouth, Isaac Johnson, Esq. and the Lady Arabella on board," was answered by three loud and hearty shouts of welcome. A tall, dignified looking lady descended from the vessel, and scarcely had the exclamations, "My dear Mary," and "My dear Lady Arabella," escaped their lips, ere they were fast locked in each other's arms.

"Come," said Mary, "I know you will be glad to enter any dwelling, after this voyage; and my dear mother will be impatient to be introduced to you."

"Then she is yet spared?" asked Mrs. Johnson.

"Yes," replied Mary; "but she is sinking away, like a decaying lamp."

"This is my mother," continued she, as she entered and placed Lady Arabella's hand within Mrs. Conant's.

"I am glad to welcome you to New England, Lady Arabella," said the mother; "though perhaps we have both been used to better apartments," added she, as her eye glanced round the humble room, with a look of pride, which ill assorted with her broken fortunes.

"No doubt, no doubt, Lady Mary," answered her guest; "but there are strong hands and firm hearts, as well as noble blood, engaged in this cause. I have heard my husband say that our own mighty kingdom was once a remote province of the Roman empire,— and who knows whereunto these small beginnings may arrive?"

"It's little that I have to do with the thoughts of kings, empires, and nobles in these days," replied Mrs. Conant; "but I would fain ask whether the old man, my father, is yet alive?"

Hobomok

"The Earl of Rivers is alive and well," said the Lady Arabella. "When my chest arrives I can give you some further news."

"Well, Madam Conant," said Mr. Johnson, whom Mr. Conant introduced a few moments after, "I have taken the liberty of bringing my lady hither; inas—much as there are no conveniences for us at Shawmut, whither we propose shortly to depart. Lady Arabella chose the rather to abide with you, on account of her sometime acquaintance with your daughter."

"Right glad we are to have a hand in helping forward the work of the Lord," replied Mr. Conant.

"Such as we have, we gladly give unto you," interrupted his wife; "but you see our velvet cushionsare wooden benches, and our tapestry the rough bark of the forest tree. However, 'it is better to be a door—keeper in the house of the Lord, than to dwell in the tents of the wicked.' "

"And is Mary cheerful under all these privations?" inquired Mr. Johnson. "Two or three years' residence so far from the busy world hath made her matronly before her time. Bless me, Lady Arabella, what would the Earl of Lincoln say to see his young favorite now?"

"How I wish I could see him," said Mary. "Is he married?"

"No," answered Mrs. Johnson; "but he is shortly to be united to the virtuous daughter of Lord Say; and a great blessing she will prove to our family, no doubt. It is said that Lord Say and Lord Brook are thinking of a settlement in New England."

"Yes," said her husband, "many godly men are turning their faces hitherward; and many of the wealthy and noble of our land are devoting their riches to the building up of Zion."

"And no doubt they'll be prospered," rejoined Mr. Conant. " 'Media movent bonitate finis.' Well may they come out of England, when Episcopacy hath become such a religious jewel in the state that the king will sell all his coronets, caps of honor, and blue garters, for six and twenty cloth caps. And who cannot see the tempter which hath led him astray? I am bold to say, Mr. Johnson, that though the king sitteth highest on the bench, his papistical queen sitteth in a chair above; and though he is placed in the saddle, she hath her hand upon the bridle."

"Yes," replied his guest, "it is a great pity that 'no bishop, no king' hath become such an oraculous truth with him, that he is willing to pawn his crown and life thereupon. His oppression gallops so hard, that it outstrips the patience of his subjects; but it is well for princes to remember that preces et lachrymœ are not the only weapons of the people. Have you heard that bishop Laud is made Chancellor of Oxford?"

"Assuredly I have not," answered Mr. Conant; "and well pleased should I be, never to have heard thereof; but it is plain enough to see that there is nothing to which he and my Lord Treasurer Weston may not aspire in the kingdom. What is to become of poor old England, when the despotic Lewis and the subtle Richelieu have so powerful an emissary in the very bosom of king Charles?"

"It's a dolorous truth indeed," replied Mr. Johnson. "But as I was saying, the Bishop of London came to the vacancy last April; and even before I departed, he straightway instituted copes, railings, and crucifixes within the university. St. Katherine's church, which was repaired as late as bishop Mountain's time, must likewise be closed, until his successor or seeth fit to revive the ceremony of consecration therein; which he did, with many popish ceremonies; such as bowing and kneeling before the altar, wearing of hood and surplice, and so on; but the worst of the whole blasphemy you have yet to hear. As Laud approached the doors of the church, his attendants opened them wide, crying with a loud voice, 'Open, ye everlasting gates, that the King of Glory may come in.' "

"No doubt this was like sugar in the mouth of the queen," rejoined Mr. Conant. "If the church of England, as it is in these days, be not the whorish woman of Babylon, I declare it requireth more than ordinary spirit of discerning to distinguish between them. Peradventure it may be the second beast, seen by St. John, who 'exerciseth all the power of the one beforehim, and causeth the earth and them which dwell therein, to worship the first beast whose deadly wound was healed.' "

"There is much reason to fear that 'God will soon put in his sickle and gather the vine of the earth, to cast into the great wine–press of his wrath,' " observed Mr. Johnson. "I am glad that I have come out from among them; and I have no doubt we shall go on to complete the good work, though there are enemies on every side—yea, though Morton, and divers others, daily increase in zeal against us."

"Charles Brown found there was a Phinehas among us, to stand up and stay the plague," said Mr. Conant; "and no doubt he hath wielded his sword in the ranks of our adversaries?"

"I understand the testimony of Mr. Brown hath always been honorable to the colonies," answered Mr. Johnson; "and as for the mischief intended by others, he who discovered the plottings of the Assyrian king, even in his bed chamber, will no doubt turn it aside."

Mary's face flushed with conscious triumph, at this mention of her lover's honorable conduct; and even her father was surprised into something like respect. However, that unyielding pride, which was at once the source of his greatest virtues and his greatest faults, prevented his making any reply.

"Well," said Mr. Johnson, after a moment's pause, "how do you succeed, outwardly and spiritually, in this heritage?"

"We speed as we can, as men must, who are no better shod," rejoined Mr. Conant. "As for worldly wisdom, we have been obliged to pay pretty roundly to dame experience for filling our heads with a little of her active after–wit; and as for the church, sects are springing up among us, like vipers in the sun.Many an honest mind hath been led away by sore temptations, and embittered by constant disputations."

"Weak wine becometh sour by fermentation, and strong wine is made better," replied Mr. Johnson. "I marvel if the Lord often suffereth the devices of Satan to lead away those who are firm in the faith;— I believe they are strengthened thereby. After all, most of the carping and controversy in the world is about matters of small moment, which tend much to the neglecting of the soul's salvation. 'Tis like unto a man's diving into a well to see the stars in broad sunlight."

"And what hath he for his pains, but to be blinded when he cometh from thence?" said Mr. Conant. "The fact is, passengers to heaven are in haste, and will walk one way or the other. If a man doubts of his way, Satan is always ready at hand to help him to a new set of opinions at every stage; and if his infernal Majesty hath too much employment, he can always find helpers in such like men as Mr. Graves and Mr. Blackstone."

Hobomok

"Do you have any trouble with the latter gentleman, now–a–days?" asked Mr. Johnson.

"I know nothing concerning him," answered Mr. Conant, "except that he came hither at the instigation of Jeroboam son of Nebat, and that he made Israel to sin. I'll tell you a very singular story, Mr. Johnson, wherein the Lord shewed his indignation against the pride of prelacy. This Mr. Blackstone, living immured there at Tri–Mountain, hath not much communication with any one on the earth or above it; but those who have been within his dwelling, say that he hath many books, forgetting the excellent advice of Pliny, 'Multum legendum est, non multa.' This man, in the sinful pride of his heart, had the book of common prayer, that dud of the devil, boundup with the Testament of our blessed Lord. Now look at the miraculous manner in which God pointed out his sin unto him. There were many rats in the room wherein these books lay, but among three hundred, none were touched save the one I have mentioned. No, not even the Testament which was bound therewith. But the book of common prayer was probably savory to such filthy vermin, for it was clean devoured."

"And had he no prickings of conscience on the occasion?" inquired Mr. Johnson.

"I doubt whether the minions of Babylon have a conscience," rejoined Mr. Conant. "If so be they have, you might as well skin a flint, as stick a pin therein."

"It is a matter of rejoicing that they are all in the hands of the Lord," observed Mr. Johnson. "In due time, he will no doubt 'drive the Canaanite out of the land.' "

"There is no reason to despair thereof," replied Mr. Conant; "but I marvel that England, which hath always been the staple of truth to the whole world, doth not rise and give him a helping hand. And now I think on't, can you tell me how the Protestant cause goes on in Europe?"

"You have heard of the success of Ferdinand the II. He has overrun all Saxony, and seems like to subdue the Protestants entirely. Urban hath swords and pens enough in his unrighteous service. Powerful kings are fighting in his cause; the Jesuits are stretching their arms north, south, east, and west, to hold up the reins of the falling church—and king Charles has caught the beast, and christened it Episcopacy, a cunning way, truly, to save him from the pursuit of his enemies. But Gustavus dares to stand out firmly against him; and I understand he is even now in arms, at the call of the reformers."

Hobomok

"I wish he had plenty of such men as Governor Endicott among his army," replied Mr. Conant. "Though I am verily sorry that there is likely to be difficulty concerning what he hath said of the king's popish colors. Assuredly I am of his opinion that it is a sinful and shameful abomination among us. The Governor is a bold man, and withal discreet. He sheweth that he hath the fear of God in this matter, though he hath none for man or devil."

"And yet," said Mary, "he is very courteous, and when he unbends the bow, you would think loving was all his trade. But come, Lady Arabella, your breakfast is, at last, ready. I have honored you more than we ever did any guests in America, for see mother's damask cloth is spread over our pine table."

"I have come into the wilderness too," rejoined her friend; "and I must learn to eat hominy and milk, and forget the substantial plum puddings of England. But 'sweet is a dinner of herbs where love is,' " said she, as her eye rested on her husband, with all the pride of woman's affection. She touched a sensitive chord, and Mary hastily turned away, to conceal the starting tears.

"Come, move to the table, Mr. Johnson," said her father; "and you too, Lady Arabella; and after we have craved a blessing thereon, we will partake of pilgrims' fare."

"I am sure this venison is good enough for an alderman," observed his guest. "Will you taste some, Lady Arabella?" .

"No, thank you," answered his wife. "I am going to try some of Mary's pumpkin and milk."

"That's right, Lady Arabella," rejoined Mr. Conant. "They are a kind of food which has beenmuch despised, but I trust hereafter nobody will speak disrespectfully of pumpkins, inasmuch as it hath pleased the Lord to feed his people thereupon for many years. Ah, Mr. Johnson, you have come among us in good time, for the Dutch ships you heard us speak of, not only brought comforting tidings from our godly brethren in the Netherlands, but likewise much that was needful for the sustenance of the body. But the time has been when our bread was measured out to us, and scanty weight too. And comfortless as you may think this hut looketh now, it hath been far worse; for there was a season that we had no doors wherewithal to keep out the Indians—but though their hunters used to come in

86

among us, 'very mooch hungry,' as they would say, the Lord so disposed them, that they never harmed a hair of our heads."

Mr. Johnson looked at his wife, and smiled half mournfully, as if he was doubtful whether she could endure such trials; but he met the answering smile of a mind aware of its difficulties, and fortified against them.

"I have heard great reports about Hobomok," said she, turning to Mr. Conant. "They say he is a clever Indian and comely withal, and that he hath been of great use to our Plymouth brethren."

"You must ask Mary about him," replied Mrs. Conant, smiling. "She loves to hear his long stories about the Iroquois, which he learned of one of their chiefs who came hither many years ago; and his account of the ancestors of some neighboring tribe, who, as he saith, were dropped by an eagle on an island to the south."

"It's little I mind his heathenish stories," rejoined her husband; "but I have sat by the hour together, and gazed on his well fared face, till the tears have come into mine eyes, that the Lord should have raisedus up so good a friend among the savages. Good morning to your honor," continued he, as Governor Endicott entered. "I trust you have not come to take our guests from us?"

"I have come in behalf of my good woman," answered the Governor, after he had returned the salutation of the strangers, "entreating that the Lady Arabella will abide with us during her stay in Salem."

"I shall most assuredly see madam Endicott, before I depart from hence," replied the noble lady; "but I chose the rather to abide with Lady Mary, as long as my husband seeth fit I should sojourn here, inasmuch as her daughter and I were some time acquainted across the water."

"It shall be as your ladyship says," rejoined the Governor; "but there are many godly women at my house, who came with you, and right glad should I be to have you added to them. At any event, I must carry away your good husband for the present, forasmuch as I have many important things whereof to inquire."

The gentlemen rose, and prepared to depart, and the ladies having returned the formal salutations of the courteous chief magistrate, were soon left to themselves.

CHAP. XIV.

```
        _____Epistles, wet ·
With tears that trickled down the writer's cheeks
Fast as the periods from his fluent quill,
Or charg'd with am'rous sighs of absent swains.
   — Cowper
```

On this day there was business and rejoicing through every corner of the settlement. Among all the daring souls, who left honor, comfort, and independence, for the sake of worshipping God according to the dictates of their own consciences, there was no one more highly or more deservedly respected than Mr. Johnson. In the bloom of life, a gentleman, a scholar, and nearly allied to a noble family, he left his own wise, wealthy, and happy land, to join a poor, despised, and almost discouraged remnant in this western wilderness. Could his prophetic eye have foreseen that the wild and desolate peninsula where he first purchased, would become the proud and populous emporium of six flourishing states; could he have realized that the transfer of government from London to Massachusetts, was but the embryo of political powers, which were so soon to be developed before the gaze of anxious and astonished Europe; how great would have been the reward of the high–minded Englishman. But his self–denying virtue had not these powerful excitements. Who in those days of poverty and gloom, could have possessed a wand mighty enough to remove the veil which hid the American empire from the sight? Who would have believed that in two hundred years from that dismal period, the matured, majestic, and unrivalled beauty of England, would be nearly equalled by a daughter, blushing into life with all the impetuosity of youthful vigor? But though Johnson and his associates could not foresee the result of the first move which they were unconsciously making in the great game of nations—a game which has ever since kept kings in constant check—he, at least, was amply rewarded by an approving conscience, and the confiding admiration of his brethren, which almost amounted to idolatry. All was life and activity during the day of his arrival. In one place might be seen boats, passing and repassing from the vessel, the ripples breaking against their oars, as they glistened in the sun. In another, the hearty interchange of salutation between seamen and landsmen; or a group of gentlemen, busy in the delivery of letters, and already eagerly engaged in discussions concerning the extent of the government wherewith they had been entrusted.

While all this bustle was going on without doors, there were questions enough to be asked and answered by the female inmates of Mr. Conant's dwelling. Several hours past before the Lady Arabella's chest was brought on shore; and though Mary's heart was throbbing high with expectation, she made no inquiries concerning letters from England. At length, however, a sailor arrived with the long expected treasures.

"This is from your father, Lady Mary," said Mrs. Johnson as she placed a letter in her hand. With provoking delay, she handed another package to Mary, as she said, "This is from brother George."

It was a neat edition of Spenser's Fairy Queen, written within, in his lordship's own hand, "To Miss Mary Conant. This cometh to remind her of bye past daies, from her olde friende George—Earl Lincoln."

"And this," continued Lady Arabella, "is likewise from Earl Rivers, who desired that Mary would open it in her own apartment."

Every one acquainted with the mazes of love, is aware of a strange perversity in the female heart with regard to such matters. Mary half suspected that her friend noticed the painful suffusion which covered her face and neck, and the package which she supposed contained news, to her more important than any thing else in the world, was placed in her little bedroom with affected indifference, and was not touched till every article of household work was completed with even more deliberate neatness than usual. Not so Mrs. Conant—she eagerly caught her letter, and tearing open the envelope, devoured with painful pleasure the only words which her father had addressed to her since her marriage. They were as follows:

"Deare Daughtere,

"Manie thoughts crowde into my hearte, when I take upp my pen to write to you. Straightwaye my deare wife, long in her grave, cometh before me, and bringeth the remembrance of your owne babie face, as you sometime lay suckling in her arms. The bloode of anciente men floweth slow, and the edge of feeling groweth blunte: but heavie thoughts will rise on the surface of the colde streame, and memorie will probe the wounded hearte with her sharpe lancett. There hath been much wronge betweene us, my deare childe, and I feel that I trode too harshlie on your young hearte: but it maye nott be mended. I have had many kinde thoughts of you, though I have locked them up with the keye of pride. The visit of Mr. Brown was very grievious unto me, inasmuch as he tolde me more certainly than I had known before.that you were going downe to the grave. Well, my childe, 'it is a bourne from whence no traveller returns.' My hande trembleth while I write this, and I feel that I too am hastening thither. Maye we meete in eternitie. The tears dropp on the paper when I think we shall meete no more in time. Give my fervente love to Mary. She is too sweete a blossom to bloome in the deserte. Mr. Brown tolde me much that grieved me to hear. He is a man of porte and parts, and peradventure she maye see the time when her dutie and inclination will meete together. The greye hairs of her olde Grandefather maye be laide in the duste before that time; but she will finde he hath nott forgotten her sweete countenance and gratious behaviour. I am gladd you have founde a kinde helpe—meete in Mr. Conant. May God prosper him according as he hath dealte affectionately with my childe. Forgive your olde father as freelie as he forgiveth you. And nowe, God in his mercie bless you, dere childe of my youthe. Farewell.

"Your Affectionate fathere, "Rivers."

"N.B. I have sente you a Bible, (which please to accept as a token of love) by Mr. Isaac Johnson; whome I esteeme a right honorable gentleman, though it grieveth me to see the worthies and nobles of the lande giving their countenance to the sinn of Non—conformitie."

The unqualified kindness of her repenting father proved too much for the weak nerves of his disobedient child; and for a long time Mary and her friend hung over her in a fearful anxiety, lest the blow should hasten a departure, which they all saw must soon come. Lady Arabella brought forward somecordials which she had brought with her, and presently her highly excited system sunk exhausted into slumber. Mrs. Johnson laid herself down beside the sleeping invalid, and gladly sought repose after the fatigue of a long and wearisome voyage. Mary willingly improved this opportunity to examine the contents of her package. A prayer book, bound in the utmost elegance of the times, first met her view. It was ornamented with gold clasps, richly chased; the one representing the head of king Charles, the other the handsome features of his French queen; and the inside of both adorned with the arms of England. Mary hardly paused to look at the valuable present in her eagerness to read the following lines.

Hobomok

"Deare Mary,

"How many times I should have written to you, could I have devised any waye for it to come safely into your hands, I leave your own hearte to judge. God knoweth howe much more I have beene in the deserte since I came hither, than while I was in the wildernesse of Newe England. It was a trial I needed, to showe me howe very deare you were unto my soule. I often think of the sicknesse, wante, and misery I founde you in, when Hobomok first guided me from Plymouth to Naumkeak; and although since the company hathe sente many vessels, there hathe been an alteration in the state of affairs, yet my hearte is readie to burste when I thinke to what you are nowe exposed. God willing, I would have shared any difficulties with you, soe as I might have called you wife; but I loved you the better in that you forgot not your dutie to your mother in your love for me. I live only on the hope of againe seeing the lighte of your countenance, but I nowe feare it cannot be until a yeare from hence. Before this reacheth you, I shall be on my waye to the East Indies, where wealthe promiseth to pour forth many treasures. For your sake I will toyle for the glittering duste, and many hardships would I endure so as I might throwe it at your feete, and saye, 'Tis all for thee. Your grandfather received your letter with much kindnesse. He spoke with greate love, of your mother, but made no remarks concerning your father. He shooke his head mournfully when I parted from him, and saide, when he was in the grave peradventure you would finde you had not been forgotten by the olde Earle: and he added, 'I hope you will live long and be happie together.' You see there is no need of having any heavy thoughts; for in the Spring I shall return unto you, if God spares my life: and whenever it pleaseth him to take your goode mother (and I sincerely hope it be not soone, much as I desire to call you mine), you will come and share my home, in England or America, as circumstances may be. To that home your father will alwayes have a wellcome, and if he chooseth not to accept it, I know nott that your dutie extendeth furthere. Some time or other I maye make New England my abode. My hearte woulde incline to staye here; but England, like the pelican we have read of, is mangling her owne bosome: though unlike that birde, she doth not give nourishment to her childrene. The Protestants banished by Mary, thirste for the bloode of Charles; sending out their poisoned arrows from Geneva and the Netherlands with all the acrimonie of exile. Our goode king Charles and his beautiful consorte are perplexed and embarrassed on every side, and it needeth no very keene eye to see that a terrible crisis draweth neare. For these reasons I would fain seeke tranquillity on the other side of the vaste ocean, if so be that an Episcopalian dove, flying from the deluge which he seeth approaching, and bringing an olive branch in his mouthe, maye there finde refuge. My hearte bleedeth for olde England, torne with religious commotions, as she hath beene, from the time of the second Tudor: but my feeble hande may not stop her wounds, gushing though they be at every pore. In the Spring I shall more certainlie knowe concerning what I have mentioned in general terms: but wheresoever I may abide, my hearte leapeth for joye, when I think I shall then be permitted to kiss your hande. I have sent a pipe to Hobomok, inasmuch as I thoughte it mighte please him to knowe that I remembered him in the big island across the water. In remembrance of our last interview at dame Willet's, I have likewise sent her a Bible, which I thought she would value more than anything wherewith I coulde furnish her. And to you my dear girle, I sende what I knowe will be more wellcome than anything but myself. Remember me kindly to Sally and dame Willet, and with much dutifull love to your mother. I remaine through life,

"Your affectionate and humble servante, "Charles Brown."

A pipe gaudily decorated, and carefully enveloped in several wrappings of paper, accompanied this package. Another contained a largely lettered Bible, written within "For my olde friende Mistress Willet." On the outside of the third parcel was written, "I had almoste forgotten my promise to Sally: if she be at Plimouth, sende this to her." It contained a handsome gown, which Brown had once playfully promised her for a wedding dress. A letter from the Earl of Rivers was bound up with the prayer book which he sent to his "Deare grandedaughtere;" but the import of it was so similar to her mother's, that I forbear tocopy it. Last of all, though the first opened, was a miniature likeness of Brown; and Mary gazed upon it till the eyes seemed laughing and beaming, in all the brilliancy of life, then turned away and wept that the mockery of the pencil had such power to cheat the heart. There was a strange contrast between these presents, and every thing around them. A small rough box placed upon a trunk, was all Mary's toilette. And now there reposed upon it the miniature of her lover, in its glittering enclosure; and a splendid prayer-book printed for the royal family. As Mary looked upon them, and thought of her present situation, she felt that it was ill-judged kindness thus forcibly to remind her of what she had left. Her meditations were interrupted by the sound of Lady Arabella's footsteps, and she hastily removed the rich articles which covered her table. However, the precaution was needless; for Mr. Johnson and his wife were perfectly aware of Brown's reciprocated attachment; and both supposed that the earl's private parcel contained intelligence from him. No one could have more conscientious horror of the form of church worship established by the first defender of the faith, and either from opinion or policy, supported by three successive monarchs; but personal respect for Mr.

Brown, and affectionate interest in Mary, overcame in some degree the narrow prejudices of the times, and the secret was faithfully preserved.

In the evening Mr. Johnson brought up another package from the Earl of Rivers. It contained, as he had mentioned, a large, handsome Bible, written within, in the trembling hand of age, "For my beloved daughtere, the Ladye Mary." Beneath, a blistered spot announced that the name had aroused the cold sympathies of advanced years, and given to the stainless page the peace–offering of a father's heart. Itwere but mockery of nature's power, to define the complicated tissue of pain and pleasure, in the mind of mother or daughter. Even the stern nerves of Mr. Conant relaxed a little, when he read the old gentleman's letter. He turned to the window, and drummed a psalm tune for a few moments, then cast round an inquiring glance, too see if any one had noticed this moment of weakness. He met the anxious look of Mary, who was timidly watching the changes of his countenance. From his softened mood she argued that her grandfather's expressions concerning Brown, had met with no very unfavorable reception; but however the old man's worldly pride might have been affected by such honorable mention of his name, it was all concealed, beneath a deep shade of rigidity, as he said,

"I have but two things whereof to complain,—the one in the letter, the other in the book; and they are both things which my soul hateth. I mean the standing of the Apocrypha in the Bible, and what is said concerning that son of Belial."

CHAP. XV.

```
        Her eye still beams unwonted fires,
With a woman's love and a saint's desires;
And her last, fond, lingering look is given
To the love she leaves, and then to heaven,—
As if she would bear that love away,
To a purer world and a brighter day.
    — Percival
```

During several weeks Mr. Johnson continued almost constantly at Shawmut* and Tri–Mountain, full of zeal and perseverance in his new enterprise. Lady Arabella in the mean time remained at Salem, and entered with enthusiasm into all the plans of her honored husband. She never spoke of the reverse in her situation, and scarcely seemed to think of it. Her character was indeed all that her countenance indicated. The expression of her eyes was gentle, but her high forehead, aquiline nose, and the peculiar construction of her mouth, all spoke intellect and fortitude, rather than tenderness. Firmness of purpose had been her leading trait from childhood; and now she tasked it to the utmost. But it was soon evident that the soul, in the consciousness of its strength, had too heavily taxed its frail, earth–born companion. The decline of each day witnessed a bright, shadowy spot upon her cheek, too delicate to be placed there by the pencil of health—her lips grew pale—and her eyes had lost all their lustre, save a transient beam of tenderness when she welcomed the return of her beloved partner. These changes could not escape the watchfuleye of affection. The important business in which Mr. Johnson was engaged, rendered his frequent presence at Shawmut absolutely necessary; but notwithstanding the solitary and wearisome distance between them, evening seldom returned without seeing him by the side of Lady Arabella. Mrs. Conant too was fast drooping, and there seemed but a hair's breadth between her and the grave. It was interesting to observe the contrast between the two invalids. One, always weak and gentle, bended to the blast, and seemed to ask support from every thing around her. The other, struggling against decay, seemed rather to give assistance, than to require it. Their husbands watched over them, with the tender solicitude of a mother over her sickening infant. Mr. Conant, stern as he was, felt that a sigh or groan from the woman whom he had so long and sincerely loved, had power to stir up those deep recesses of feeling, which had for years been sealed within his soul; and Mary's heart was ready to burst with keen and protracted anguish, when she saw death standing with suspended dart, taking slow, but certain aim, at two endeared victims. But medicine, anxiety, and kindness, were alike unavailing; and soon they both retired to the same apartment, and laid themselves down on the beds from which they were never more to rise. Their feeble hold upon life daily grew more precarious, till at length nothing could tempt their anxious husbands from the pillow. Neither of them had spoken much for several days, when on the 24th of August the faint voice of Mrs. Conant was heard, as she whispered,

"Roger—My dear Roger."

In a moment he was at her side.

"What would you say, Mary?" asked he.

"There are many things I would have spoken," shereplied; "but I fear I have not strength wherewith to utter them. If Brown comes back, you must remember our own thwarted

94

love, and deal kindly with Mary. She hath been a good child; and verily the God who had mercy on our unconverted souls, will not forsake her. Will you promise?"

"I will," answered the old man, in an agitated voice. "Verily, my dear wife, your dying request shall be obeyed."

"I would fain turn to the light," said she, "for I feel that my departure draweth nigh."

Mary and her father gently raised her, and turned her toward the little window. She looked on her husband, with the celestial smile of a dying saint, as she said,

"I die happy in the Lord Jesus. Sometimes I would fain tarry longer for your sake; but the Lord's will be done."

The agonized man pressed back the crowding tears, as he said,

"If in the roughness of my nature, I have sometimes spoken too harshly; say that you forgive me."

"I have nothing to forgive," she replied. "To me you have been uniformly kind."

She reached out her hand to Mary—"For my sake," added she, "be as dutiful to your good father as you have been to me."

"I will—I will," answered Mary, as she, sobbing, hid her face in the bedclothes.

She spoke no more for several hours. At length, Mr. Conant, who remained close by her side, heard her whisper, in low and broken tones, "My dear husband." She attempted to extend her hand toward him, but the blindness of death was upon her, and it feebly sunk down by her side. As her husband placed it within his, she murmured, "I cannot see you, dear Roger. Kiss me before I die." He stooped down—and oh, how deeply painful was that last embrace. Mary likewise bent over her, and kissed her cold cheek.

"My child—God—bless"—was heard from the lips of that dying mother; but the utterance was troubled and indistinct. Her breathings soon became shorter and more disturbed, and the last agonies seemed passing over her. No sound was heard in the room, till presently a short, quick gasp announced the soul's departure. Mr. Conant placed his hand upon her heart—its pulse no longer throbbed. He held the taper before her mouth—no breath was there to move the steady flame. Mary uttered an involuntary shriek, and sunk upon her knees. There is nothing like the chamber of death to still the turbulence of passion, and overcome the loftiness of pride. What now was the shame of human weakness to that bereaved old man? He stood by the corpse of her, who for twenty years had lain in his bosom, and he heeded not that the big, bright tears fell fast upon the bed. Nothing now remained but the last, sad offices of friendship; and they were silently performed. Not a word was spoken by father or daughter. The sheet was carefully drawn over that pale face; and both bowed down their weary, aching heads upon the pillow, in still communion with their own souls.

During this time, the Lady Arabella had sunk into a slumber so deep and tranquil that she seemed almost like her departed companion. Mr. Johnson remained with her hand clasped in his, half doubtful whether it was not indeed the sleep of death. Towards morning she awoke; and resting her eyes upon her husband with a look of unutterable love, she feebly returned the pressure of his hand, as she said,

"You are always near me, dear Isaac." After a thoughtful pause, she asked, "Is not the Lady Mary dead?"

"She is," answered Mr. Johnson.

"Assuredly I so thought," continued she. "I dreamed that angels came for her, and she said they must wait for me. They are standing by her bed–side now. Don't you see the light of their garments? Well, I shall soon be ready."

"My God, my God," exclaimed the young husband, "would that the bitterness of this cup might pass from me."

"But it may not pass," rejoined his wife, calmly; "and you must drink it like a christian. Let your whole trust be on the Rock of Ages."

"I could bear all, Arabella," replied he, "had I not brought you into trials too mighty for your strength. But for my selfish love, you might now be living in ease and comfort."

Hobomok

"My dear Isaac, does this sound like a follower of the Lamb?" said she. "The time of my departure hath come, and what matters it whether it be in England or America? In the short space we have been allowed to sojourn together, I have enjoyed more than all my life beside; and let this remembrance comfort you when I am gone. Remember me most kindly to my good brother. May his earthly union be as happy and more permanent than mine."

For a long time she seemed exhausted by the effort she had made. Then, taking the ring from her finger,

"Give this to Mary" said she; "and when she looks thereon, bid her think to what all human enjoyment must come. I know you will always wear my miniature. It would have been a great comfort, had I been permitted to leave a living image of myself; but it hath pleased the Lord to order otherwise. Faint not in the enterprise whereunto our blessed Lord has called you; and remember we meet again in Jesus."

The heart of her husband was too full to speak; and he could only kiss her emaciated hand in reply. She fixed her dying gaze upon him, and a faint smile hovered round her lips, shedding its unearthly light over her whole countenance, as she said, "I hear the angels singing. 'Tis time for me to go." Her look was still towards her husband, when her lids closed as if in peaceful slumber. All was hushed. The flickering lamp of life was extinguished.

There, in that miserable room, lay the descendants of two noble houses. Both alike victims to what has always been the source of woman's greatest misery— love—deep and unwearied love. The Lady Mary had in her life time been so still and fair, that the smile on her placid countenance seemed but a mockery of death; and whoever looked upon the Lady Arabella would have judged that thought was still busy beneath those closed eye–lids.

The next day all was still in that house of mourning. Each one spoke in a subdued tone, and moved with light and cautious tread, as if fearful of awakening the repose of the dead. All had passed a sleepless night, and as they arose from the pillow which had for hours received their tears, a silent grasp of the hand, strong in the first desperation of grief, was their only salutation.

Hobomok

"My friend," said Mr. Conant, "it becometh not christians to be cast down in time of tribulation. Let us pray to Him who is always a present help in time of trouble."

Mary handed down the Bible; and her father read the 88th Psalm, without evincing any other emotionthan the slight quivering of his lip and the gathering moisture of his eye. Mr. Johnson rose to prayer, and for awhile his voice was clear and undisturbed; but in a few moments sobs were alone audible. Even his exalted piety sunk in that dreadful conflict of feeling. One burst of weakness, earth claimed as its own—the rest he gave to heaven. His brethren were all eager to speak words of comfort. He thanked them for their kindness, and tried to hear them calmly; but the mourner only can tell how painful at such seasons, are well–meant offers of consolation.

Few honors could there be paid to deceased nobility. The bodies were placed in rough coffins, covered with black, and supported side by side, even as they had expired. The procession stopped on a neighbouring eminence, and after Mr. Higginson had dwelt long on the sufferings and virtues of the departed, the earth closed over them forever.

Grief, like all violent emotions, is still when deepest. Mr. Johnson returned from that sad funeral, and not a sigh or tear was seen to escape him. The next day, he went to Shawmut, mingled in the debates of his associates, encouraged the settlers, and surveyed the tract he had purchased at Tri–Mountain. How to build up the church seemed to occupy his whole thoughts; and to that purpose he directed his active and constant exertions. But in the midst of this artificial strength, it was plain enough to be seen, that his heart was broken.

A few weeks after Lady Arabella's death, he was seen slowly proceeding through the forest, on his way to Salem. He paused not to rest his weary footsteps till he reached the place where he had last seen the features of his adored wife. Silently he laid down his head upon the ground, and wept. He arose, and for awhile rested his melancholy gaze on the brightsun and verdant earth. Then kneeling beside the grave, he prayed, "Heavenly Father, I beseech thee to forgive this worship of an earthly idol; and if it so pleaseth thee, take me from this world of sin and misery."

He entered Mr. Conant's dwelling, and slightly partook of the food which Mary's assiduous kindness prepared for him. No expostulations could prevail upon him to remain through the following day. He retraced his solitary path to Shawmut, and it soon became evident that the hand of death was upon him.

The day before his decease, he called Governor Winthrop to his bed–side.

"Let not the laborers of the vineyard mourn that I am removed," said he. "Tell them to go on, like brave soldiers of Christ Jesus, until they perfect the work wherewithal he hath entrusted them. I bless the Lord that he has called me to lay down my life in his service, inasmuch as he has suffered me to witness the gathering of one church in apostolic purity. I have but one request to make unto you. Bury me in the lot which I have laid out at Tri–Mountain;* that at the great judgment–day I may rise among the heritage which I have feebly endeavored to build up. I would fain have the Lady Arabella placed by my side; but it is a wearisome ways to Salem, and wheresoever our bodies may be, our souls will be united. God forgive me, if in sinful weakness, I have loved that dear woman even better than his righteous cause."

The excellent man soon after followed his young wife to the mansions of eternal rest; and on the same day that the news arrived at Salem, the pious and reveredMr. Higginson was likewise numbered with the dead. Misfortunes and discouragements seemed crowding upon the infant colonies, which had so lately been rejoicing at their prosperity and increase. "In all their streets was the voice of lamentation and wo." The countenances of men became disconsolate, and mournfully they passed each other, as they said, "Ichabod! Ichabod! Verily the Lord hath sorely smitten us."

CHAP. XVI.

```
Nor think to village swains alone
Are these unearthly terrors known;
For not to rank nor sex confined
Is this vain ague of the mind.
    — Rokeby
```

Independent of universal public depression, a peculiar and settled gloom pervaded Mr. Conant's dwelling; and on every account it was a sad home for one in the freshness of existence. True, Mr. Conant seldom spoke with his former harshness, and even the tones of his voice had become more gentle; still his feelings were too rigid and exclusive to sympathize with a young heart almost discouraged by surrounding difficulties. One after an another, she had been deprived of the cheering influence of Sally Oldham, the firm support of Lady Arabella, and the mild, soothing spirit of her mother; and no one was left to supply their place. As for Mrs. Oldham, the whole circle of her ideas might be comprised in one sentence, viz. "People will marry whom they are fore–ordainedto marry, and die when they are appointed to die." The facetiousness of Mr. Oldham was sometimes amusing; but his feelings were blunt, and his wit too often partook of coarseness and vulgarity. There were some in the settlement in whom Mary might have found as much sympathy as she ever met from her old associate, but she knew them not; and when the heart is oppressed with many sorrows, it shrinks from the task of initiating a stranger into all its mysteries of thought and feeling. With none therefore, had Mary any thing like communion. Even Hobomok came unnoticed, and went away unheeded. Sometimes she would think of asking her father's permission to return to England; and then the prospect of Brown's arrival the ensuing spring, would determine her to await his motions. This hope enabled her to discharge her daily duties with tolerable cheerfulness; but twilight generally saw the melancholy maiden seated by her mother's grave. At such seasons her imagination would be busy with the light, silvery clouds, as they hurried along the sky in every variety of form and hue. In one place might be seen a group rising side by side, like the sacred groves of the ancients; here, a stupendous column stood alone, like the magnificent pillar of some ruined edifice; and there, a large, shadowy cloud rested upon the horizon, like the aerial drapery of an angel's couch. It was a mild evening at the commencement of October, when, as she had seated herself as usual to pursue this fanciful amusement, her attention was suddenly arrested by the singular appearance of one of those capricious forms. It was a vessel—so perfect and distinct that the shrouds seemed creaking in the wind, and the canvass fluttering to the breeze. It slowly floated along the atmosphere, till it came over the place whe she stood, when it gradually descended and meltedinto air. Mary had no small share of the superstition of the times, and shuddering at the fatal omen she hastily ran to inform her father. The figure was again seen in the west, and to Mr. Conant, it seemed even more plain than it had to his daughter. Mr. Oldham and two or three neighbours were now called in; and a third time did the strange appearance rise, sink, and disperse, even as at first.

"I marvel if some mishap be not about to befall the shipping which is coming hither," said Mr. Conant. "Forerunners like this, seldom appear but to warn us of some coming disaster."

"That's true enough," rejoined Mr. Oldham. "Don't you remember the story that Capt. Thurston told us about the Castor and Pollux lights on the mast of the Jewel, the night before she run against the Ambrose? A sad mishap that. They say the Jewel would assuredly have been torn in pieces, had it not been for the discreet counsel of Mr. Johnson. God rest his soul; he was the wisest and best man in the whole fleet; and no disparagement to them who are left behind."

"Them Castor and Pollux lights are bad things when one of them is seen alone," quoth another; "but they are nothing to what I have seen and heard in the line of forewarnings. The night before the godly Mr. Higginson died, I heard the tolling of a bell by the hour together, as plain as if I had been within bow–shot of St. Paul's."

"I'm thinking it could be no bell in this world that echoed in this wilderness," replied Mr. Oldham; "unless the devil is sexton now–a–days, and has the ringing of their English bells, which I trow is no very unlikely thing, while Bishop Laud sitteth at the helm."

"It's not well to use lightness of speech concerning such things," said his companion. "I knew a man in England who laughed at the power which it hath pleased the Lord to give unto Satan, and the self–same night a blow was heard on the side of his house as loud as a clap of thunder, and it was cracked to the very foundation, though none of his neighbours heard the report thereof."

"England has come to a dreadful pass in these days," observed Mr. Conant. "I have known some of their scholars who would fain judge of the doings of their Maker by their own reason, and they say that all such like things are the cunning devices of man's imagination."

"I should like to have such folks see a sight that I can tell them of," said a third. "On the night that Mr. Johnson died, though he was at Shawmut, and of course I couldn't know that his end drew near, I saw a light on the foot of my bed, about two in the morning. It burned a few minutes, and then went out. My wife straightway said 'You may depend upon it, the pious Mr. Johnson hath departed,' and sure enough, as nigh as I can discover, he died just at that time."

The relation of such wonders continued for a long time, and perhaps would never have known an end, had not the lateness of the hour reminded them it was time to depart.

There is a great facility in appropriating any thing uncommon to our own situation and circumstances. Mary readily believed that the extraordinary phantom was meant for herself only; and she immediately conjectured it foreboded evil tidings from her lover. The more she indulged these thoughts, the more their power increased, till their unquiet influence entirely deprived her of rest. At that credulous period, it is not surprising that superstition exerted her full force over a mind so prone to revel in the etherial visions of imagination. And who, even in these enlightened days, when reason sits almost sole arbiter of the human mind, has not felt similar influences powerful and strong within him? Who among the wisest and the best, has not experienced states of feeling when the light sigh of the summer breeze, or the gentle pattering of midnight rain, or mayhap a passing shadow on the moonlight floor, or the rustling of the trees, as they bowed their foliage to the evening gale, has had power to quicken the pulse, and restrain the motion of the breath? But there are moments of weakness, which pride would hardly deign to bring before the tribunal of reason; and which, if brought there, would doubtless be found to originate in causes merely physical. Whatever is their source, they sometimes come suddenly upon the mind, striking with magic force, "the electric chain wherewith it's darkly bound;" and in this instance, Mary's fearful augury was too soon realized. The next week Hobomok came to Salem, bearing a letter for Mr. Conant, and another for Governor Endicott. The first contained information of the death of Earl Rivers, written by his grandson; the other mentioned that an East India ship had been lately wrecked, with the loss of her whole crew and cargo; and added that Charles Brown, formerly of Salem, was among the passengers. No sooner had the news passed the lips of the Governor, than it spread through the whole settlement, like an electric shock through an united circle. The circumstance of Mary's attachment was well known, and the matrons and maidens paid a passing tribute of grief, as they asked,

"How will the poor damsel bear this? The Lord support her; for whatsoever be her errors in doctrine,she hath a sweet–favored face, and a disposition like an angel."

"Hold your blasphemous tongues," replied their rigid listeners. "Because the children of Belial have a comely form, a smooth skin, and noble blood, you forsooth straightway liken them to angels of light. Wot you not that all these things pass away as if they had never been? As for the untimely end of him who hath bred so much disturbance among us, 'tis but the visitation of the Lord, for his sinful upholding of the domineering prelates."

While people were busy with similar observations, an officious neighbour eagerly carried the unwelcome news to Mary.

For a moment her heart reeled, and the blow threatened to suspend her faculties. The next, there was a ray of hope. She had become accustomed to false alarms, and she trusted this would prove to be one. Fallacious as she felt this hope, she could not, and would not relinquish it. Whatever were her feelings, they were but briefly exposed to the unfeeling curiosity of her guest. Her father's supper was left half prepared, her cloak hastily thrown on, and an instant after, she entered Governor Endicott's.

"The Lord help you," exclaimed Mrs. Endicott, "how pale you look, and how you tremble. Do be seated, and let me give you some cordial."

"Has his Honor received a letter from England?" inquired the anxious girl, without taking notice of her kind offer.

"Bless your young heart," replied Mrs. Endicott, as she put the corner of her apron to her eyes, "I'm expecting him home every minute. But do take a drop of cordial. It grieves me to death to see you look so."

Her importunities were all useless, and the good woman would have attempted words of comfort, had not the misery of Mary's countenance made such an emphatic appeal to her forbearance. Mary spoke not; but fixed her wild and anxious gaze on the door, until the Governor entered, when she suddenly rose and inquired.

"Have you received a letter from Plymouth to day?"

She had always been a great favorite with the chief magistrate, for, zealous as he was, he was not the man to look on so fair and young a creature, and hate her for her creed. Her question awakened his deepest sympathy, and he cast a pitying glance upon her, as he replied,

"It is all too true, Mary."

There are things which the heart can never realize, be they ever so long in prospect. Come when they will, they come with crushing, agonizing power. The mother may listen for weeks, to the hushed moan of her dying infant; the bridegroom may watch the hectic flush, daily settling more deeply on the cheek of his young bride; but the chain is rivetted closer and closer, and terrible must be the force which rends it asunder.

Mary answered not. She pressed her hand hard upon her brow, and she who had been so gentle and childlike that a rough word would draw tears from her eyes, now neither wept nor sighed. She was about to depart, but the Governor grasped her hand affectionately as he said,

"Forgive me, my good girl, I know that your heart is full; but I would fain remind you that we are only sojourners in this world until we can find a better; and that whatsoever befalleth us, is meant for oureternal good. Cast therefore the burthen of your sorrows at the feet of Jesus."

Mary appreciated his kindness, but she could not attend to him; and, struggling to release her hand, she muttered an indistinct answer, and hastily quitted the house, to hide her grief from his view. She rested her head on a young tree which grew in the path, and tried to pray; but, in that whirl of feeling, she could not even think, and scarcely knowing what she did, she proceeded homeward.

Her father had finished his supper, and though he had found it unprepared, he uttered no complaint. He well knew the occasion of this neglect; and his own thoughts were not unmixed with bitterness. Conscience, cool and unbiassed, inquired whether he had not in some measure mistaken obstinacy and pride for conscientious zeal; and in the humbleness of the moment, he acknowledged that christians were too apt to mistake the voice of selfishness for the voice of God. His earliest enemies had been of the English church, and he had seen his wife drooping and dying amid the poverty which his religious opinions had brought upon her, and yet he tried hard to be convinced, and did at last verily believe, that earthly motives had nothing to do with his hatred of Episcopacy. He still retained all his abhorrence of Brown's sentiments, but since the death of his wife, he had thought, with a good deal of concealed pleasure, how very graciously he would make a sacrifice to the peace of her only child; and now that there was no hope of making this atonement for his past harshness, he felt more of disappointment than he would have been willing to acknowledge. In this softened state of feeling, one gentle expostulation would have driven him to the bosom of his child, there to impart comfort, and seek forgiveness. He did indeed speak feelinglyof the death of her grandfather, and told her of the God who was alike the support of the young and the aged. While he dwelt upon the excellence of religious consolation, he called her "my dear child," and more than once his eyes filled with tears. Unfortunately, Mary was too absent, too distressed, to receive these tardy proofs of affection with the gratitude which kindness was always wont to excite; so after one or two efforts to mention the painful subject, he did as he too often had done—stifled the voice of nature, and hid all his better feelings beneath the cold mask of austerity. Mary, tortured with thoughts she could no longer endure in his presence, observed that she was going to dame Willet's, and then left him to his meditations.

CHAP. XVII.

```
The tempter speaks, when all is still,
And phantoms in the mind will raise,
That haunt the path of after days.
* * * * * *
On one sad night she left her home;
She parted with the tawny chief,
And left me lonely in my grief.
     — Yamoyden
```

The same restlessness which had led Mary to dame Willet's, soon made that scene of former happiness insupportable. The loquacious old woman did not understand the nature of the human heart so well as the friends of Job, who "sat down on the ground, and none spake a word to him; for they saw that his grief was very great." Mary could not endure thegood dame's blunt sympathy; beside, every object which there met her view, did but remind her of her lover's farewell interview; so she drew her cloak around her, and prepared to depart. The old lady followed her, and gently taking hold of her arm, looked in her face as if fearful of expressing her doubts.

"Mary," said she, "I have done all I could to comfort you; but verily, my dear child, I fear you are not altogether yourself."

"Assuredly I am," replied Mary; "but I cannot stay here, for when I stand at that little window, it seems as if I could see him as he looked the last time I ever saw him."

Notwithstanding this declaration, there was a partial derangement of Mary's faculties. A bewilderment of despair that almost amounted to insanity. She sat down by her mother's grave, and wished to weep. The sorrow that can be exhausted, however keen it may be, has something of luxury in it, compared with grief when her fountains are all sealed, and her stormy waters are dashing and foaming within the soul. Mary's heart refused to overflow, and she laid down her head on the cold sod, in hopes it would cool the burning agony of her brain. As she sat thus, insensible of the autumnal chilliness, she felt something lightly thrown over her. She looked up, and perceived that it was Hobomok, who had covered her with his blanket, and silently removed a short distance from her. He approached when he saw her rise.

"It's a cold night for Mary to be on the graves," said he.

"Ah, Hobomok," she replied, "I shall soon be in my own grave."

The savage turned away his head for some time, as if struggling with some violent emotion.

"How Hobomok wish he could make you happy," at length said he.

There was a chaos in Mary's mind;—a dim twilight, which had at first made all objects shadowy, and which was rapidly darkening into misery, almost insensible of its source. The sudden stroke which had dashed from her lips the long promised cup of joy, had almost hurled reason from his throne. What now had life to offer? If she went to England, those for whom she most wished to return, were dead. If she remained in America, what communion could she have with those around her? Even Hobomok, whose language was brief, figurative, and poetic, and whose nature was unwarped by the artifices of civilized life, was far preferable to them. She remembered the idolatry he had always paid her, and in the desolation of the moment, she felt as if he was the only being in the wide world who was left to love her. With this, came the recollection of his appearance in the mystic circle. A broken and confused mass followed; in which a sense of sudden bereavement, deep and bitter reproaches against her father, and a blind belief in fatality were alone conspicuous. In the midst of this whirlwind of thoughts and passions, she turned suddenly towards the Indian, as she said,

"I will be your wife, Hobomok, if you love me."

"Hobomok has loved you many long moons," replied he; "but he loved like as he loves the Great Spirit."

"Then meet me at my window an hour hence," said she, "and be ready to convey me to Plymouth."

Hobomok

She returned home; and Hobomok, overjoyed at this unexpected fortune, prepared to obey her injunctions. Her father was absent when she entered, and lighting a taper, she sat down in the solitary room, and alternately attempted to fix her attention on the prayer book and Bible. In a few moments Mr. Conant returned. He spoke but little; but his prayer that evening evinced much parental tenderness as well as lofty piety. Fervently did he beseech that God would heal the wounded and broken heart, and lead back all those who were wandering in errors to the true fold of Christ Jesus.

When Mary thought that she was perhaps hearing that venerable voice for the last time, her heart relented. She acknowledged that a sort of desperate resentment towards him, had partly influenced her late conduct; and she asked herself,

"What if he has been harsh and restrained in his intercourse with me? It is cruel to wrench from him his last earthly tie; and to prostrate the soul of a parent, because my own lies bleeding in the dust."

Perhaps this effort of dawning reason and gentler feeling would have prevailed; but her father angrily seized the prayer book, which she had carelessly left in his way, and would have thrown it upon the fire, had she not caught his arm and rescued it from his grasp.

"Have it out of my sight," exclaimed the old man, in a violent tone. "My soul abhorreth it, as it doth the spirits of the bottomless pit."

That single act decided the fluctuating fate of his child. Who can look back upon all the important events of his life, without acknowledging that the balance of destiny has sometimes been weighed down by the most trivial touch of circumstance. Mary's mind was just in that vacillating state when a breath would have turned her from her purpose, or confirmed it forever. Her heart writhing and convulsed as it was, was gentle still; and it now craved one look of tenderness, one expression of love. That soothing influence she in vain sought; and the feelings which had harrowed up her soul to that fatal resolution, again returned in their full force. In the unreasonableness of mingled grief and anger, she accused her father as the sole cause of her present misery; and again she sunk under the stupifying influence of an ill directed belief in the decrees of heaven, and the utter fruitlessness of all human endeavour. It was strange that trouble had power to excite her quiet spirit to so much irascibility; and powerful indeed must have been the superstition, which could induce so much beauty and refinement, even in a moment of desperation, to exchange the social band, stern and dark as it was, for the company of savages. Mary retired to her own room, resolved on immediate departure; but she was not sufficiently collected to make any necessary arrangements; she even neglected taking a change of apparel. However, Brown's miniature was not forgotten; and as it lay before her, she could think of nothing, only that the form, which once could boast so much dignified beauty, was now unshrouded and uncoffined in the deep, deep ocean,—and imagination shuddered over the thoughts which followed. She placed the miniature in her bosom, and looked out upon the scenes she was so soon to leave. Her eye first rested upon Endicott's Hollow, where, as she supposed, it had been first revealed to her that Hobomok was to be her husband; and falling on her knees,

"Oh, Charles," murmured she, "if thy pure spirit is looking down upon this action, forgive me, in that I do but submit to my fate."

Presently the low whistle of Hobomok was heard. She obeyed the signal, and in a few moments she was by his side, walking toward the seashore. Almost every thing in their path was, in some way or other, connected with Brown; and she would frequently pause, as she uttered some mournful and incoherent soliloquy. The Indian had witnessed the dreadful ruins of mind in his own tribe, and the fear of her insanity more than once occurred to him; then again her brief answers to his questions would be so prompt and rational, that he could not admit the doubt.

"She is communing with the Good Spirit," thought he.

And now might be seen the dark chieftain seated in his boat, exulting in his prize, and rowing with his whole strength, while the rays of a bright October moon shone full upon the contrast of their countenances. Neither of them spoke, save when Hobomok stooped on his oar, and drawing the blanket more closely around her, asked whether or not the cold was uncomfortable. He would often raise his loud, clear voice in some devotional boat–song, alternately English or Indian, among which the following seemed to be a favorite.

"Lend me, oh, moon, lend me thy light, that I may go back to my wigwam, and my wakon bird may rest there in safety. I will rise with the sun, to see his fire consume the morning couds. I will come back to my wakon–bird, laden with beaver and deer."

Hobomok

The whole scene was singularly melancholy. Nothing but the face of the Indian wore an expression of gladness. Mary, so pale and motionless, might have seemed like a being from another world, had not her wild, frenzied look revealed too much of human wretchedness. The moon, it is true, pursued her heavenly path as bright and tranquil as ever; but the passing clouds made her appear hurried and perturbed, even as the passions of men float before the mild rays of the Gospel, making them seem as troubled and capricious as their own. Nature too, was in her saddest robe; and the breeze, as it swept along the variegated foliage, sounded like the dismal roarings of the distantocean. Mary's meditations were more dull, and cold, and dreary still. It is difficult to tell what the feelings could have been, half bewildered as they were, which led her to persevere in so strange a purpose. It is even doubtful if their victim could have defined them. But whatever they were, they were endured and cherished, until the boat drew up on the shore of Plymouth. Fortunately for Hobomok, none of the inhabitants had risen, and he guided her to his wigwam unobserved. In a few words, he explained to his mother the occasion of the visit. Full of astonishment, the grateful squaw danced, sung, and caressed Mary, with every demonstration of frantic joy. Hobomok endeavoured to calm her transports, and urged the necessity of forwarding the marriage immediately; for the savage had many fears that Mary would yet shrink from the strange nuptials. His arguments were readily assented to, and Hobomok asked his intended bride whether she was willing to be married in the Indian form.

"Yes," answered she, and turned from him, as if a sudden pang had passed through her heart.

"She is mad," whispered the old squaw.

Her son hesitated a moment, then taking some wine, which Governor Bradford had once given his sick mother, he offered it to her, as he said,

"If Mary sick, this will make her well."

"I am not sick," was the laconic reply.

Hobomok again convinced of her rationality, went forth to make arrangements for his marriage. In the course of an hour, he returned with four of his relations. They spoke no English, but each one lifted his hands as he looked at Mary, and seemed to utter some exclamation of surprise. Presently they joined in a dance, singing in a low tone, for fear of exciting the suspicion of their white neighbours. After this was concluded, Hobomok stept out, and looked cautiously in every direction, to see that none were approaching, then taking Mary by the hand, he led her round the wigwam, and again entered. In the mean time, a mat had been placed in the centre of the room, and thither the Indian led his bride. The eldest of the company then presented him with a witch–hazel wand of considerable length, and having placed one end of it in Mary's hand, the bridegroom stood waiting for the ceremony. The oldest Indian then uttered some short harangues, in which he dwelt upon the duty of a husband to hunt plenty of deer for his wife, to love her, and try to make her happy; and that the wife should love her husband, and cook his venison well, that he might come home to his wigwam with a light heart. To this Hobomok responded in a tone half way between singing and speaking,

"Hobomok love her like as better than himself. Nobody but Great Spirit know how well he loveth her."

The priest then looked toward Mary, as if waiting for her answer.

"Tell how well you love him," said the Indian woman, as she touched her arm. Mary raised her head with a look, which had in it much of the frightful expression of one walking in his sleep, as she replied,

"I love him better than any body living."

Hobomok then took the rod, which they had held, and breaking it into five pieces, gave one to each of the witnesses. The married couple still continued standing, and the company formed a circle and danced round them three times, singing their marriage song. When this was finished, Hobomok took out his pipe and handed it to the priest. It was the one which Brown had sent, and when Mary saw it, she uttered a piercing shriek, as she pointed to it, and said, "Send it away! Send it away!" Her husband understood her meaning, and returning it to his pocket, he produced another. After each one had smoked, they again formed a ring, and danced and sung as before, each one, as he came near the door, dancing backward, and disappearing. After they had all gone, Hobomok went out and buried Brown's beautiful present in the earth. Mary continued listless and unmoved, apparently unconscious of any change in her situation. But the ceremony of that morning was past recall; and Mary Conant was indeed the wife of Hobomok.

CHAP. XVIII.

It was strange for him to show
Such outward signs of inward wo.
    — Yamoyden

The next morning Mr. Conant arose, and, as usual, went out to his labors. He came in at his accustomed time, and found that no preparations had been made for their scanty morning meal. He knocked at Mary's door. No one answered. With dreadful apprehension he looked into her apartment. The lifeless object which he had expected, did not meet his view; and he saw at a single glance, that the bed had been unoccupied. A suspicion even more painful than the first, then flashed upon him, that his child had been driven to suicide. "Oh God," thought he, "have I likewise been called to offer my last remaining child upon thine altar." Then came the question, "Might I not have performed the work of the Lord as well, and shown less rigour to that poor thoughtless girl?" He felt that he had, in reality, known very little of Mary, except through the medium of her mother; and he now blamed himself that he had not given her his confidence and sympathy, instead of compelling her so cautiously to conceal her feelings. The words of his dying wife seemed to resound in his ears, as she said, "Be kind to Mary for my sake;" and with this remembrance came the sting of self−reproach, the keenest that can enter the human soul. For a few moments the old man sat down, and rested his head upon his hand, with more positive wretchedness than he had ever before felt, crushed as his heart had been in the battle of life. He stood for some time hesitating between the consciousness that something must be done, and a perplexity as to what course to pursue. At length the idea that she might have slept at Mr. Oldham's, or Dame Willet's, occurred to his mind, and though he gave it little credence, it afforded a moment's relief.

Mr. Conant had persevered in his resolution to continue at Naumkeak, when but three of his discontented companions remained to share his poverty, and even those three threatened to desert him; when his family, unable to endure such hardships, were obliged to consent to a temporary separation; and when his young, vigorous boys were bowed down to the grave by labor and famine. In the midst of all these difficulties, the MS. states that "he made a vow to abide in Naumkeake as long as the Lorde pleased to spare his life, if he coulde finde a clam on the seacoaste, or an acorne on the trees." This same inflexible self−command had ever since made him the "very soul of counsel," in all times of danger; and it now induced him to chasten his heart, that its agitatedfeelings might not be betrayed to the wondering gaze of his neighbours. With his usual calm appearance he entered Mr. Oldham's dwelling, and inquired whether they had seen any thing of Mary the preceding night.

"Bless me, no," answered Mrs. Oldham. "I may safely say she has scarcely darkened my doors since the day Sally was married. But is she missing, Goodman?"

Mr. Conant briefly answered that she had not slept at home, and went out as he added,

"Peradventure she abode with Dame Willet."

"Poor man," said Mrs. Oldham. "I always knowed it would be so, from the very minute I heard of Brown's death. I said then she'd never live through it. There never any good come of crossing folks in love, to my knowledge. I'm sure I never would have said a word, if Sally had taken it into her head to marry a Pequod."

"I'm sure I would, though," rejoined her husband. "A pretty piece of business it would be of a truth, to have a parcel of tawny grandchildren at your heels, squeaking powaw, and sheshikwee, and the devil knoweth what all."

"I hope you don't mean that folks have a free will of their own in such matters," said his wife.

"To be sure I do. 'Tan't much that I should have done in the business, if I hadn't had my own way," rejoined he. "But now I have made out to get on my boots, I'll go out and inquire concerning this matter. Mary was as sweet a creature as ever man looked upon; and if she be indeed missing, the boats must be had out."

"You're a sinful wicked man to talk, considering you're a christian," said his wife, as he departed.

The application at dame Willet's was equally unsuccessful, and the report that Mary Conant was dead, spread like wildfire through the village. She had been so humble, kind, and cheerful among them, and had so seldom evinced any aversion to their sentiments, that she was a universal favorite. The young admired her as the loveliest being they had ever beheld; and the old, even while they held up her errors of doctrine as a warning to their children, could not refrain from adding,

"Assuredly, in many things she hath borne herself worthy of a woman professing godliness."

For some minutes, the settlement was one scene of commotion.

"Have out the boats—have out the boats," said one.

"Fire guns over the water," said another.

These orders were complied with, and boats were ordered out in several directions. As Mr. Oldham was entering one of these, he espied a ring lying close to the water's edge, and stepping back, he asked Mr. Conant if he had ever seen it.

"The Lady Arabella gave it to my child," answered the disconsolate father; and without further pause he passed through the crowd, who readily made way for him. He entered his desolate home, fastened the door of his little apartment, and threw himself down beside the bed. Hours passed away before the bitterness of affliction could be in any degree overcome; but at length the tears flowed plentifully, and fervently did he pray for support and assistance, to that God who had never forsaken him in his hour of need.

In the meantime the search of his brethren had of course proved useless, though the supposition that Mary was drowned amounted almost to absolute certainty. Now that the opinion was apparently so well proved, every one, as usual, had something to give as additional evidence. Mrs. Endicott made exaggerated reports of the wildness and paleness of her looks, when she came to inquire concerning the letter. Another remembered to have seen her go to her mother's grave at sun–down, and remain there till after the night closed in.

"For my part," says Dame Willet, "I couldn't go quietly to my bed till I went up and looked into Mr. Conant's to see that Mary was at home with her father; for she came down to my house in the evening, and she took hold of my hand till I thought it had been in a vice and she had a dreadful wild look about her. Poor creature, I couldn't help foreboding that all was not right, when she sighed so, and said that she little thought my house was the last place where she should ever see him; for you must know," continued she, "I gave the young folks a meeting without Goodman Conant's knowing of the same."

"And you should take shame and sorrow to yourself for such an action," replied Mr. Skelton. "I grant the maiden had many charms, and much seeming goodness in speech and behaviour, but so had that idolatrous woman of the house of Stuart, whom it pleased the Lord, in his righteousness, to bring to the block. I tell you, woman, the Most High will visit their iniquity upon the heads of all such as bow the knee to Baal, and worship the golden calf of Episcopacy. Wot ye not that Mr. Conant was led by the fear of God in this matter?"

"Assuredly I think so," answered the dame; "but a body couldn't look upon the girl without loving her, and I meant no harm, your Reverence."

"I don't suppose you did, good woman; but it behoves us to give little heed to natural affection, when we are engaged in the work of the Lord Jesus. Forasmuchas it seems useless to waste more time and powder in this melancholy search, I will even go up and speak a word to Mr. Conant, in his troubles; though I doubt not he bears them like a christian."

When Mr. Skelton arrived on his errand of consolation, he distinctly heard the voice of his friend as he prayed,

"If in this thing, O Lord, I have acted from my own pride, rather than from zeal for thy glory, I beseech thee, spare me not—but pour out the vials of thy wrath upon my unworthy head, so that the sins of my child may be forgiven."

The voice ceased—and a few moments after Mr. Skelton knocked for admission. No answer was returned, until he said,

"I have come to see you, Mr. Conant, thinking it might comfort you to unite in prayer during this season of distress."

"I have much reason to thank you," replied Mr. Conant; "but I trust your Reverence will not be offended if I tell you that I would fain be left with God and my own heart for a season."

Before evening Mr. Conant had regained his wonted manner. All his necessary avocations were performed, and at night he went into Mr. Oldham's and said with his customary calmness, "I will partake of whatever you have for supper, if you are so inclined;" and at nine o'clock he performed the family devotions, in a voice so distinct and untroubled, that all who heard him wondered at the strength wherewith it pleased the Lord to support him. But quiet as all seemed on that unruffled surface, there was a tempest beneath, which threatened to uptear the very roots of existence; and even when his lips were opened in prayer at the footstool of divine grace, his thoughts were deep in the cold wave. Whatever were his concealedfeelings, before three days had elapsed, none could judge by the most trifling external sign, that the waters of affliction had passed over him. During this time, he had invited Dame Willet and her son Jacob to take up their abode at his house, and they now constituted his whole family. On the third evening after Mary's departure, the good woman and her son were absent, and Mr. Conant seated alone by his solitary fire, when Mr. Collier arrived at Mr. Oldham's, bringing news of the lamentable fact. All were eager to ascertain how, when, and where, it had been discovered.

"It's a dismal story to tell her old father," observed Mr. Collier; "but my good woman hath seen her with her own eyes, and heard her acknowledge that she was married to Hobomok, so there can be no mistake about it. Our knowledge of the matter came after this fashion. Sally went in to see Hobomok's mother, as is often her custom, inasmuch as she is old, and frequently alone. The squaw had stept out when she first went in; but seeing somebody in the bed, Sally thought she had been sick, and so went up to speak to her, when behold, she found it was Mary Conant. She said she was so stupid that she did not seem to know her, and she wouldn't speak a word; only when she asked if what the old squaw said, was true, she answered, Yes. My good woman came home and went to bed sick about it, and she desired me straightway to come up and deliver the tidings."

Considerable altercation ensued, concerning who should inform Mr. Conant. Mr. Oldham and his wife were as eager to undertake the unwelcome task, as their son-in-law was willing to decline it. Mr. Oldham was just preparing to execute the mission, when Mr. Skelton entered, and having heard the story, heput an end to all interfering claims, by saying that he thought it was his duty to impart the same.

As Mr. Conant sat alone, ruminating on the many sad events in his chequered life, a few reluctant tears had forced their way, and lay cold and undisturbed upon his furrowed cheek. Perhaps had he known the near approach of his minister, they had never been shed; as it was, they were hastily brushed away, when he returned the pressure of his hand.

"I'm glad to see you have borne this heavy affliction as becomes a follower of Christ Jesus," said Mr. Skelton.

"It doth but cause our enemies to blaspheme, when christians, who of all men ought to glory in affliction, are disposed to murmur at the weight thereof," replied Mr. Conant. "Whatsoever dispensation the Lord may send in his anger, I hope he will always give me strength to say, 'My trust is in thee, and in the shadow of thy wings will I take refuge.' Besides, Mr. Skelton, how would it beseem me to talk of my own sorrows, when the Lord hath so sorely smitten us all?"

"Of a truth," rejoined the clergyman, "he hath removed many goodly pillars from the land. Much could I wish that the godly Mr. Higginson were alive this day; inasmuch as he had a soul–ravishing, a soulsaving, and a soul–comforting speech. Alas, that he left not his mantle behind him."

"No doubt he was taken away from the evil to come," answered Mr. Conant. "But we have abundant need of his pious reproofs among us, notwithstanding you carry yourself much for the edification of those unto whom you are called to minister. These are trying times among us. Numbers are swept off by sickness; and the blight and mildew in our corn seemeth to forbode a famine; and as for the colonyat Shawmut, I verily fear, their joyful beginning will have but a dolorous end."

"If every man bears his part of the public calamities as well as you have borne the death of your child, I have no doubt the Lord will smile upon our undertakings; though for a season 'He feedeth us with the bread of tears, and giveth us tears to drink in great measure,'" rejoined Mr. Skelton.

"Why, I trust, I have not in vain heard your godly exhortations from the pulpit," said Mr. Conant; "nor yet the dying admonitions of Mr. Higginson, who told us in all times of trouble to lean upon the Lord of Hosts. Verily I will rest upon His promises, though 'mine own familiar friend, in whom my soul trusted, who did eat of my bread, should lift up his heel against me;' yea, though 'lover and friend be put far from me, and mine acquaintance into darkness."'

"But what would you say," asked Mr. Skelton, "if Mary was yet alive?"

"What would I say?" exclaimed he, starting up eagerly. Then with more composure he added, "Verily, I would thank the Lord, in that the bitter cup had passed from me. Have you heard any news?"

"Mary is alive and well at Plymouth," answered Mr. Skelton.

"God be praised," said Mr. Conant—and now indeed the tears fell fast and unrestrained. He seized Mr. Skelton's hand, and repeated again and again, "The Lord be praised—The Lord be praised for all his goodness."

A stern, unbending sense of duty, a gloomy experience of human nothingness, all his strange obliquities of character had left him a father still. The clergyman said nothing to interrupt this burst of feeling, until Mr. Conant paused and inquired,

"But why went she thither without my knowledge?"

"That is what will be the hardest for you to bear like a christian," rejoined Mr. Skelton; "and I would not tell you thereof till you have strengthened your mind for the worst."

"I can bear any thing, if so be she is alive," answered the distressed father. "I beseech you, let me hear the worst."

"She is married to Hobomok," replied Mr. Skelton.

The unexpected information fell like a deadly blow on the heart of the old man; and those cheeks and lips grew pale, which no man had ever before seen blanched since his boyhood. He stood at the window a moment, firmly compressing his lips, to keep back some choking emotion; but finding the effort ineffectual, he took up his hat and went forth to seek a solitude where he might pour out his sorrows before his Maker. An hour elapsed before he returned, and could Mary have foreknown the agony of that hour, she had never left the parental roof. When he again entered his house, he found his friend still waiting for his return. He took his offered hand, as he said,

Hobomok

"I am more calm now, Sir. God forgive me, if in aught I have rebelled against his holy will; but assuredly I find I could more readily have covered her sweet face with the clods, than bear this; but the Lord's will be done."

"It behoves you to think what would have become of her unconverted soul if she had died in such a state," replied the minister. "Goodman Collier thinks she was bereaved of reason, when she did this deed; and peradventure the Lord may yet raise her up to be 'a burning and a shining light.'"

"For her soul's salvation, God grant she may not be in her right mind," answered Mr. Conant. "I would fain have the poor stray lamb returned to the fold."

"Had you no suspicions concerning Hobomok's visits heretofore?" asked Mr. Skelton.

"I knew he was grateful to us for much we had done for him at Plymouth," rejoined Mr. Conant; "but verily, had I been told it extended further, I had never believed so unlikely a thing. I knew that Mary loved to hear his long stories, abounding as they were with metaphors, but then the thoughtless child was always given to vain imaginations, which profit not. Her good mother told me, the day before she died, that Mary's heart would always hanker after him who is now lost in the bowels of the ocean; and I promised that I would give my assent to their marriage. Peradventure this chastisement hath come upon me, because I thought in my heart, to countenance the doings of the unrighteous."

"Well," replied Mr. Skelton, "it is a mercy to receive the reward of our sins, in some sort, during this life; but you must not be tempted to forget Him in whom you said you would put your trust, 'though darkness overshadowed you, and the waters compassed you about.'"

Mr. Conant shook his head despairingly. "I had made up my mind to her watery grave," said he; "but to have her lie in the bosom of a savage, and mingle her prayers with a heathen, who knoweth not God, is hard for a father's heart to endure."

"Let us unite in prayer," said Mr. Skelton. "Verily at all seasons it is the best balm for a wounded soul."

Mr. Conant was indeed soothed and strengthened by the exercise. The next day saw him busy in hisdaily employments;—weeks and months past on, and witnessed the same unvaried fortitude. But the heart of the old man was bowed down within him. The widow Willet said, she often heard him groan bitterly in the night; and his neighbours frequently noticed him leaning upon his axe or his hoe, by the hour together, apparently lost in melancholy reflections.

CHAP. XIX.

```
Yes—it was love—if thoughts of tenderness,
Tried in temptation, strengthened by distress—
Which nor defeated hope, nor baffled wile,
Could render sullen, were she ne'er to smile,
Nor rage could fire, nor sickness fret to vent
On her one murmur of his discontent—
If there be love in mortals—this was love!
    — Byron
```

For several weeks Mary remained in the same stupified state in which she had been at the time of her marriage. She would lie through the livelong day, unless she was requested to rise; and once risen, nothing could induce her to change her posture. Language has no power to shadow forth her feelings as she gradually awoke to a sense of her situation. But there is a happy propensity in the human mind to step as lightly as possible on the thorns which infest a path we are compelled to tread. It is only when there is room for hope, that evils are impatiently borne. Desolate as Mary's lot might seem, it was not without its alleviations. All the kind attentions which could suggest themselves to the mind of a savage, were paid by her Indian mother. Hobomok continued the same tender reverence, he had always evinced, and he soon understood the changing expression of her countenance, till her very looks were a law. So much love could not but awaken gratitude; and Mary by degrees gave way to its influence, until she welcomed his return with something like affection. True, in her solitary hours there were reflections enough to make her wretched. Kind as Hobomok was, and rich as she found his uncultivated mind in native imagination, still the contrast between him and her departed lover, would often be remembered with sufficient bitterness. Beside this, she knew that her own nation looked upon her as lost and degraded; and, what was far worse, her own heart echoed back the charge. Hobomok's connexion with her was considered the effect of witchcraft on his part, and even he was generally avoided by his former friends. However, this evil brought its own cure. Every wound of this kind, every insult which her husband courageously endured for her sake, added romantic fervor to her increasing affection, and thus made life something more than endurable. While all her English acquaintances more or less neglected her, her old associate, Mrs. Collier, firmly and boldly stemmed the tide, and seemed resolved to do all in her power to relieve the hardships of her friend. For a long time her overtures were proudly refused; for Mary could not endure that the visits of one, who had been so vastly her inferior, should now be considered an honor and obligation. However, persevering kindness did in time overcome this feeling, and in less than a year, Sally became a frequent inmate of her wigwam. To this, was soon likely to be added another source of enjoyment. Before two years passed away, she became the mother of a hopeful son. Under such circumstances, his birth was no doubt entwinedwith many mournful associations; still the smiles of her infant brought more of pleasure than of pain. As Mary looked on the little being, which was "bone of her bone, and flesh of her flesh," she felt more love for the innocent object, than she thought she should ever again experience.

During the period before his birth, nothing occurred of any importance to our story, excepting that Mr. Conant had written two letters to his daughter. The first conjured her not to consider a marriage lawful, which had been performed in a moment of derangement, and invited her to return to the arms of a parent who tenderly loved her. The second informed her of a considerable legacy left to her by the Earl of Rivers, and again offered her a welcome home and oblivion of all the past. Mary's heart was melted at these proofs of affection, when she had so little expected them; but she well knew she should only be considered an outcast among her brethren, and she could not persuade herself that her marriage vow to the Indian was any less sacred, than any other voluntary promise. So she wrote to her father, implored his forgiveness, hinted at the deplorable state of mind which had led her to this extremity, stated many reasons which now rendered it impossible for her to return, even if she were so disposed, and concluded by urging him to appropriate her property to his own comfort, as she should probably never be in a situation to enjoy it.

After this general view of things, we must now pass over to the 16th of September, 1633, and leave the interim to the reader's imagination. The old squaw had lately died of a fever, and symptoms of the same disorder began to appear in her little grandson, now nearly two years old. On the morning we have mentioned, Mrs. Collier took her own little bloomingdaughter in her arms, and went into the wigwam to inquire concerning the health of the boy. No sooner was she steated, than the children, accustomed to see each other, began to peep in each other's faces, and look up to their mothers, their bright, laughing eyes beaming with cherub love. Hobomok entered, and for a moment stood watching with delighted attention, the bewitching sports of childhood. He caught up the infant, and placing his little feet in the centre of his hand, held him high above his head.

"My boy, my brave hunter's boy," said he, and pressing him in his arms he half suffocated him with caresses. He placed him in his mother's lap, and took down his quiver, as he said, "Hobomok must be out hunting the deer." The child jumped down upon the floor, and tottling up to him, took hold of his blanket and looked in his face, as he lisped, "Fader come back gin to see 'ittle Hobomok."

Again the father stooped and kissed him, as he answered

"Hobomok very much bad, if he didn't come back always to see little Hobomok, and his good Mary."

He went out, but soon returned and lifting the blanket, which served for a door, he again looked at his boy, who would alternately hide his head, and then reach forward to catch another glimpse of his father.

"Good bye, Hobomok—Good bye, Mary"—said the Indian. "Before the sun hides his face, I shall come home loaded with deer."

"Take care of yourself," said his wife, affectionately; "and see that Corbitant be not in your path."

"Sally, you have never said one word about my marrying Hobomok," continued she; "and I have no doubt you think I must be very miserable; but I speaktruly when I say that every day I live with that kind, noble–hearted creature, the better I love him.

"I always thought he was the best Indian I ever knew," answered Sally; "and within these three years he has altered so much, that he seems almost like an Englishman. After all, I believe matches are foreordained."

Hobomok

"I don't know concerning that," rejoined Mary. "I am sure I am happier than I ever expected to be after Charles' death, which is more than I deserve, considering I broke my promise to my dying mother, and deserted my father in his old age."

While conversation of this nature was going on at home, Hobomok was pursuing his way through the woods, whistling and singing as he went, in the joyfulness of his heart. He had proceeded near half a mile in this way, when he espied an eagle, soaring with a flight so lofty, that he seemed almost like a speck in the blue abyss above. The Indian fixed his keen eye upon him, and as he gradually lowered his flight, he made ready his arrow, and a moment after the noble bird lay fluttering at his feet.

"A true aim that, Hobomok," said a voice which sounded familiar to his ears. He raised his head to see from whence it proceeded. Charles Brown stood by his side! The countenance of the savage assumed at once the terrible, ashen hue of Indian paleness. His wounded victim was left untouched, and he hastily retreated into the thicket, casting back a fearful glance on what he supposed to be the ghost of his rival. Brown attempted to follow; but the farther he advanced, the farther the Indian retreated, his face growing paler and paler, and his knees trembling against each other in excessive terror.

"Hobomok," said the intruder, "I am a man like yourself. I suppose three years agone you heard I was dead, but it has pleased the Lord to spare me in captivity until this time, and to lead me once more to New England. The vessel which brought me hither, lieth down a mile below, but I chose the rather to be put on shore, being impatient to inquire concerning the friends I left behind. You used to be my good friend, Hobomok, and many a piece of service have you done for me. I beseech you feel of my hand, that you may know I am flesh and blood even as yourself."

After repeated assurances, the Indian timidly approached—and the certainty that Brown was indeed alive, was more dreadful to him than all the ghosts that could have been summoned from another world.

"You look as if you were sorry your old friend had returned," said the Englishman; "but do speak and tell me one thing—Is Mary Conant yet alive?"

Hobomok fixed his eyes upon him with such a strange mixture of sorrow and fierceness, that Brown laid his hand upon his rifle, half fearful his intentions were evil. At length, the

Indian answered with deliberate emphasis,

"She is both alive and well."

"I thank God," rejoined his rival. "I need not ask whether she is married?"

The savage looked earnestly and mournfully upon him, and sighed deeply, as he said,

"The handsome English bird hath for three years lain in my bosom; and her milk hath nourished the son of Hobomok."

The Englishman cast a glance of mingled doubt and despair towards the Indian, who again repeated the distressing truth. Disappointed love, a sense of degradation, perhaps something of resentment, were all mingled in a dreadful chaos of agony, within the mind of the unfortunate young man; and at that momentit was difficult to tell to which of the two, anguish had presented her most unmingled cup. The Indian gazed upon his rival, as he stood leaning his aching head against a tree; and once and again he indulged in the design of taking his life.

"No," thought he. "She was first his. Mary loves him better than she does me; for even now she prays for him in her sleep. The sacrifice must be made to her."

For a long time, however, it seemed doubtful whether he could collect sufficient fortitude to fulfil his resolution. The remembrance of the smiling wife and the little prattling boy, whom he had that morning left, came too vividly before him. It recks not now what was the mighty struggle in the mind of that dark man. He arose and touched Brown's arm, as he said,

"'Tis all true which I have told you. It is three snows since the bird came to my nest; and the Great Spirit only knows how much I have loved her. Good and kind she has been; but the heart of Mary is not with the Indian. In her sleep she talks with the Great Spirit, and the name of the white man is on her lips. Hobomok will go far off among some of the red men in the west. They will dig him a grave, and Mary may sing the marriage song in the wigwam of the Englishman."

"No," answered his astonished companion. "She is your wife. Keep her, and cherish her with tenderness. A moment ago, I expected your arrow would rid me of the life which has now become a burden. I will be as generous as you have been. I will return from whence I came, and bear my sorrows as I may. Let Mary never know that I am alive. Love her, and be happy."

"The purpose of an Indian is seldom changed," replied Hobomok. "My tracks will soon be seen far beyond the back–bone of the Great Spirit. For Mary's sake I have borne the hatred of the Yengees, the scorn of my tribe, and the insults of my enemy. And now, I will be buried among strangers, and none shall black their faces for the unknown chief. When the light sinks behind the hills, see that Corbitant be not near my wigwam; for that hawk has often been flying round my nest. Be kind to my boy."—His voice choked, and the tears fell bright and fast. He hastily wiped them away as he added, "You have seen the first and last tears that Hobomok will ever shed. Ask Mary to pray for me—that when I die, I may go to the Englishman's God, where I may hunt beaver with little Hobomok, and count my beavers for Mary."

Before Brown had time to reply, he plunged into the thicket and disappeared. He moved on with astonishing speed, till he was aware he must be beyond the reach of pursuit; then throwing himself upon the grass, most earnestly did he hope that the arrow of Corbitant would do the office it had long sought, and wreck upon his head deep and certain vengeance. But the weapon of his enemy came not. He was reserved for a fate that had more of wretchedness. He lay thus inactive for several hours, musing on all he had enjoyed and lost. At last, he sprung upon his feet, as if stung with torture he could longer endure, and seizing his bow, he pursued with delirious eagerness every animal which came within his view.

The sun was verging towards the western horizon, when he collected his game in one spot, and selecting the largest deer, and several of the handsomest smaller animals, he fastened them upon a pole and proceeded towards Plymouth.

It was dark, and the tapers were lighted throughout the village, when he entered Governor Winslow's dwelling. Whatever was the purpose of his visit, it was not long continued; and soon after, the deer was noiselessly deposited by the side of Mr. Collier's house, with a slip of paper fastened on his branching horns. Hobomok paused before the door of his wigwam, looked in at a small hole which admitted the light, saw Mary feeding her Indian boy from his little wooden bowl, and heard her beloved voice, as she said to her child, "Father will come home and see little Hobomok presently."

How much would that high–souled child of the forest have given for one parting embrace—one kind assurance that he should not be forgotten. Affection was tugging hard at his heart strings, and once his foot was almost on the threshold.

"No," said he; "it will distress her. The Great Spirit bless 'em both."

Without trusting another look, he hurried forward. He paused on a neighboring hill, looked toward his wigwam till his strained vision could hardly discern the object, with a bursting heart again murmured his farewell and blessing, and forever passed away from New England.

CHAP. XX.

```
God, the best maker of all marriages,
Combine your hearts in one.
    — King Henry V.
```

Charles Brown had listened with respect and admiration to the farewell address of the Indian, and forgetful of every other sentiment, he eagerly pursued him, with the intention of restoring the happiness he had so nobly sacrificed. But there were few of the swiftest animals of the forest could outstrip the speed of Hobomok. His step was soon out of hearing, and Brown having at length lost sight of his track, reluctantly gave over the pursuit. In his anxiety to overtake the savage, and in the bewilderment of his own brain, he lost the path; and the sun was nearly setting, when he regained the road he had left. He seated himself upon a rock, in hopes of again meeting Hobomok, should he attempt to return to Plymouth. No sound was heard in those lone forests, save the rustling of the leaves as they bowed to the autumnal wind, or the shriek of some solitary bird as he flapped his wings above the head of the traveller. To these was now and then added the monotonous sound of the whippowill, answered by a strain of wild and varied melody from some far–off songster of the woods. The foliage of the trees was every where so thickly interlaced, excepting the narrow footpath which opened before him, that scarcely a single ray of light could be discerned among the branches. The brightness of the sun had already gone beyond theview, and a long train of sable clouds were gathering in the west, as if mourning his departure. The conflicting feelings of the young man were settled in deep melancholy; and the aspect of nature "suited the gloomy habit of his soul."

"Thus," thought he, "has been my ambitious course. Thus did the dawning rays of hope and imagination send forth their radiance, till the world seemed all light and joy. I have struggled through the clouds which have gathered around me, cheered by the thought that Mary's love would render the evening of my days tranquil and happy. Desperate must have been the temptations which beset the dear girl's mind, when she took the cruel step which has forever wrenched that hope from me. But the deed is done, and God forbid that my resentment should rest on her unhappy head. Existence must now be as sad as those dull clouds which are so fast gathering."

The evening grew more dark, and still nothing betokened the approach of the hunter; and the dismal hooting of the owls, and the distant growling of the wolf, warned the traveller to seek safety in the haunts of men. He proceeded along his journey uninterrupted; and soon the well known wigwam of Hobomok met his view. He started with a sudden pang, and walked along rapidly, whistling lest he should hear the sound of that voice so dear to his memory. Immediately after the painful spot was passed, he met a little boy, hieing homeward, as merry and hardy as youth and poverty could make him.

"My boy," said he, "can you tell me where Mr. Collier lives?"

The child pointed to a new house that was hard by, and scampered home to tell his father there was a stranger in the settlement. Mr. Brown already had his hand upon the latch, when the recollection of Hobomok'sterror induced him to ascertain who were the inmates of the dwelling, before he ventured to enter. Stepping round cautiously he looked in at the window. Sally sat there knitting by a dim taper, her foot gently moving the white pine cradle, which contained her sleeping infant.

"I shall no doubt alarm her if I go in so suddenly," thought he.

While he was deliberating, he heard the noise of coming footsteps, and presently a man stumbled, and fell directly before him.

"What have we here?" muttered the stranger, springing on his feet and looking back. "I'll go in and ask Sally for a light."

Hobomok

"Who are you, sir?" inquired he, as he noticed Brown standing before his door.

"Mr. Collier," replied the young man, "I would not willingly alarm you, therefore give me your hand, before I tell you my name. You suppose Charles Brown to be dead, but he is alive, and you now have him by the hand."

"Charles Brown of Salem!" exclaimed Mr. Collier.

"The same," answered his visitor.

"If you are really the living Mr. Brown," said the other, "why do you stand outside of my door? Don't you suppose you'd have a welcome within, after all that's past and gone?"

This was the first expression of kindness which the disconsolate wanderer had heard since his arrival, and he shook the hand of his old acquaintance so cordially, that he could have no remaining doubts whether he was real flesh and blood.

"I knew I should frighten your wife," replied he. "I saw she was alone, and inasmuch as I knew she supposed me to be dead, I thought best to await yourreturn. But if you will prepare her to see me, I will gladly enter, for I am overcome with weariness."

Mr. Collier entered, and drawing his chair towards the cardle, he looked in upon his infant, and smiled, as he said,

"Sally, I have some strange news to tell you, if you'll promise not to be frightened."

"What is it? What is it?" asked his wife, eagerly. I'm sure you don't look as if it was very terrifying."

"It's bad enough though, for some folks that you love," replied he, thoughtfully. "Charles Brown is alive."

"Charles Brown alive!" screamed Sally. "Tell me how you know it."

"I have seen him, shook hands with him, and talked with him," rejoined her husband.

"What will poor Mary do?" asked his wife.

"That's the first thing I thought of," answered Mr. Collier. "Poor fellow, he little knoweth what is in reserve for him; but the Lord overruleth all things in infinite wisdom. I have one thing more to tell you; and you must be calm about it, for peradventure I should have been sorely frightened had I seen his face before he spoke. He standeth even now at the door."

"It can't be true," exclaimed she, jumping up, and looking out of the window.

The door opened, and Brown stood before her.

"Do you believe it now, Sally?" said he.

"Yes, I do; and I am glad to see you," she replied; "and since my good–man is here, I will kiss your hand."

She looked him in the face till the multitude of thoughts in her kind heart broke forth in tears.

"Do tell us," said Mr. Collier, "for I was so surprisedthat I never thought of it until now, how came you hither?"

"I came in an English vessel, which lies two miles below waiting for wind. My story is no uncommon one for an East India passenger. Our vessel was wrecked, and for nearly three years I have been a prisoner on the coast of Africa. How I effected my escape, I have neither strength nor spirits to tell you now."

"How wonderful are the doings of Providence," rejoined Mr. Collier; and he looked at his wife, as if he would add, "Poor fellow, his hardest fortune is yet to come."

"You need not look thus mournfully on each other, my good friends," observed the young man. "Had I not known the worst, I had not so long refrained from asking after my dear Mary."

"How could you have heard so soon?" inquired both.

Hobomok

"I met Hobomok soon after I landed," replied Brown; "and I have waited a long while, trusting to see him again as he returned; but if he came he must have taken a different route. He himself told me that Mary was his wife, and the mother of an Indian boy."

"Is it possible you have met Hobomok alone, and yet live to tell thereof?" asked Mr. Collier.

"I met him alone in the woods, and sincerely did I wish he would take my life," answered the young man. "I have a story to tell of that savage, which might make the best of us blush at our inferiority, Christians as we are; but I cannot tell it now."

"Speaking of hunting, makes me think of what I stumbled over, when I met you," replied Mr. Collier. "I'll take a light and go out to see what it was; forassuredly I thought it seemed like some large animal."

He soon returned, bringing in the pole, which had been left there by Hobomok.

"This is strange," exclaimed he. "Here is as handsome a deer as ever I put eyes on; and three clever foxes."

"What's that paper, fastened on the horns?" asked his wife.

Her husband untied it; and when opened, it proved to be as follows:

"This doth certifie that the witche hazel sticks, which were givene to the witnesses of my marriage are all burnte by my requeste: therefore by Indian laws, Hobomok and Mary Conant are divorced. And this I doe, that Mary may be happie. The same will be testified by my kinsmen Powexis, Mawhalissis, and Mackawalaw. The deere and foxes are for my goode Mary, and my boy. Maye the Englishmen's God bless them all.

The marke of Hobomok.

"Written by me, at the instigatione of the above Indian, who hath tolde me all, under an injunctione of secresie for three daies.

Edward Winslow. Governor of the jurisdictione of New Plimouth."

"His conduct is all of a piece, noble throughout," observed Brown. And he repeated to his friends, his singular interview with the Indian.

The behavior of the savage naturally drew forth many expressions of wonder and admiration; and the next question was, "How is Mary to be informed of all this? She will, no doubt, be alarmed at the absence of Hobomok."

"I am going to prepare some food for Mr. Brown," replied Sally; "and after I have done that, if you will take care of little Mary, I will go and spend the night with her. It is so near the fort, there can't be any danger when there are two of us; and perhaps to−morrow she will see Mr. Brown."

The young man insisted that he needed no food; and that he himself would stand sentinel near Mary's wigwam, and guard her through the night. Sally represented the impracticability of this plan, and the terrible alarm it would give Mary, should she chance to discover him; and after a good deal of friendly altercation, she carried her point. A small repast was set before Brown, and Mrs. Collier, having made all necessary arrangements for the comfort of her family, and having received repeated cautions, both from her husband and her guest, departed to the dwelling of her friend. She found her, as she expected, anxiously looking out for the hunter.

"What can be the reason he does not return?" said she, as Sally entered. "I was just thinking of coming in to ask you about him."

"Perhaps he did not find game plenty," replied Mrs. Collier.

"You know he seldom fails to find something," rejoined his anxious wife; "and besides he always comes home at night, whether he has been lucky or unlucky. He never would trust me and his boy to the mercy of Corbitant, after the night closed in; but perhaps, like every thing else that I ever loved, he is snatched away from me."

"I have thought a great deal of that trick you tried at Naumkeak," observed her friend. "It would bestrange if Hobomok should die, and Brown should yet return alive and well; and yet we do sometimes hear of things as wonderful as that."

Hobomok

"How wildly you talk, dear Sally," she replied. "Charles has been dead these three years, and it is wicked in me to think of him so much as I do; for if ever a wife owed love to a husband, heathen or christian, I do to Hobomok. But have you heard any thing about my husband, that made you speak thus?"

Slowly did her friend prepare her mind for the reception of the tidings, and cautiously and gradually did she impart them, until she was made to comprehend the return of her lover, his meeting with Hobomok, and the exalted course which her husband had pursued.

The singular circumstances were so prudently revealed, and Mary had been so much accustomed to excitement, that no violent tumult was raised within her bosom; but she sobbed till Mrs. Collier thought her heart must break.

"I would willingly go down to the grave," said she, "willingly forfeit my hopes of heaven, if I could know they were both happy; but to have Hobomok a wanderer, for my sake, and to have him die among strangers, without one relation to speak those words of comfort and kindness, which he has so often uttered to me, I cannot—I cannot endure it." "I only have sinned; and yet all the punishment has fallen upon his head. No; not quite all; for I know Brown must despise me."

Sally tried every gentle art to soothe her perturbed feelings, and before she departed, she extorted a promise that she would see Brown towards evening. A thousand times did Mary repent this resolution, notwithstanding her eagerness for the interview. Alternatelywould she weep, and then pray that blessings might rest on the head of him who had so lately been her husband; and if she regained any thing like composure, little Hobomok, who wandered about unused to such neglect, would ask, "What for make mamy ky so 'bout fader;" and his tone of infant melancholy would call forth all her sorrows afresh. At length the day drew toward a close; and Mary's pulse throbbed high when she heard those well–known footsteps approaching. In an instant she was at the feet of her lover, clasping his knees with a pale imploring countenance, as she said,

"Can you forgive me, Charles,—lost and humbled as I have been?"

"The Lord judge you according to your temptations, my dear Mary," replied he, as he raised her to his bosom, and wept over her in silence.

Hobomok

For a time both seemed afraid to trust each other with a second word or look.

"My temptations were many," said Mary, interrupting the silence. "I cannot tell you all now. But at home all was dark and comfortless; and when I heard you too were gone, my reason was obscured. Believe me I knew almost as little as I cared, whither I went, so as I could but escape the scenes wherewith you were connected; but to this hour, my love has never abated."

"I believe it, Mary; but where is your boy?"

The child moved before his mother, as he lisped, "Here's little Hobomok."

Mary caught him to her heart and kissed him, while the tears fell fast upon his cheeks.

"He is a brave boy," observed Brown, as he passed his fingers through the glossy black hair of the fearless young Indian.

"Those were the last words his father said to him," rejoined Mary, and she placed him in his arms, and turned away to conceal her emotion.

"Let's talk no more concerning this subject," said the young man. "The sacrifice that has been made is no doubt painful to us both; more especially to you, who have so long known his goodness; but it cannot now be remedied. You must go to Mr. Collier's to night; but will you first say that you will be my wife, either here or in England?"

"I cannot go to England," she replied. My boy would disgrace me, and I never will leave him; for love to him is the only way that I can now repay my debt of gratitude."

"What is his name?" asked Brown.

"According to the Indian custom, he took the name of his mother," answered Mary. "I called him Charles Hobomok Conant."

"He shall be my own boy," exclaimed the young man. "May God prosper me according to my kindness towards him. But, my dear Mary, will you, as soon as possible, be my wife?"

"If you do not utterly despise me," rejoined she, in an agitated tone. "You well know how dear you are to my soul."

Mary and her son removed to Mrs. Collier's; and a letter was immediately despatched to Mr. Conant, informing him of existing circumstances, and requesting that the marriage might be performed at his house. The old gentleman returned this brief answer.

"Come to my arms, by deare childe; and maye God forgive us both, in aughte wherein we have transgressed."

The necessary arrangements were made; and a few days after, Mr. Brown, accompanied by Mary andher son, returned to Salem. It was the first time Mary had seen the town since her departure with the savage; and on many accounts the meeting could not be otherwise than one of mingled pain and pleasure.

Her father clasped her in a long, affectionate embrace, and never to the day of his death, referred to a subject which was almost equally unpleasant to both. A few weeks after their arrival, Mr. Skelton was sent for, and Mary stood beside her bridegroom, her hand resting on the sleek head of that swarthy boy. He, all unconscious of what was going forward, gave little heed to the hand which was intended to restrain his restless motions; for now he would be wholly concealed behind his mother's dress, and now, one rougeish black eye would slily peep out upon his favorite companion, the laughing little Mary Collier.

Charles Brown and Mary Conant were pronounced husband and wife, in the presence of her father and Dame Willet, Mr. and Mrs. Oldham, and her two constant friends from Plymouth.

A new house was soon after erected near Mr. Conant's; and through the remainder of his life, the greater part of his evenings were spent by that fireside. Disputes on matters of opinion would sometimes arise; but Brown seldom forgot his promises of forbearance, and they were always brought to an amicable termination. Partly from consciousness of blame, and partly from a mixed feeling of compassion and affection, the little Hobomok was always a peculiar favorite with his grandfather. At his request, half the legacy of Earl Rivers was appropriated to his education. He was afterwards a distinguished graduate at Cambridge; and when he left that infant university, he departed to finish his studies in

England. His father was seldom spoken of; and by degreeshis Indian appellation was silently omitted. But the devoted, romantic love of Hobomok was never forgotten by its object; and his faithful services to the "Yengees" are still remembered with gratitude; though the tender slip which he protected, has since become a mighty tree, and the nations of the earth seek refuge beneath its branches.

THE END.